D0960685

PSYCHOANALYSIS IN TRANSITION

PSYCHOANALYSIS IN TRANSITION

A Personal View

Merton M. Gill

AP THE ANALYTIC PRESS

1994   Hillsdale, NJ   London

Published by
The Analytic Press, Inc.
365 Broadway
Hillsdale, New Jersey 07642

Library of Congress Cataloging-in-Publication Data

Gill, Merton Max, 1914—
    Psychoanalysis in transition : a personal view / Merton M. Gill.
        p. cm.
    Includes bibliographical references and index.
    ISBN 0-88163-112-4
    1. Psychoanalysis I. Title.
BF173.G496 1994
150.19'5—dc20   94-17701
                                                            CIP

Printed in the United States of America
10 9 8 7 6 5 4 3 2 1

To Ilse

Contents

Preface

I have long believed that if an author explained how a book came to be, it would be useful to the reader. So, herewith how this book came to be. Some years ago, more than I care to remember, I decided to write a textbook of psychoanalytic theory and practice. I was very dissatisfied with the available texts, especially one of the most popular ones, which I consider to be a catechism rather than a textbook. I wanted to write one that would stress the controversies in psychoanalysis and that would be of interest to experienced analysts and to beginners in the psychological therapies. For me, this includes anyone doing dynamic psychotherapy, by which I mean in this context an antonym to behavior therapy.

Somewhere I had heard that a sophisticated primer should be an introduction to a field and would encompass it in a way that would be enlightening to the expert as well as to the beginner. That is the kind of book I wanted to write.

Not surprisingly, with such an aim, I got bogged down time and again and would abandon the project for some time. Finally I achieved a manuscript of several hundred pages and sent it to Paul Stepansky, Editor-in-Chief of The Analytic Press, asking him to give me an opinion and perspective. With his usual acuity, he told me at once that I had not decided on my audience. He also suggested that the book needed to be brightened up and in particular that I give it a more personal slant.

He did not realize that he had hit a nerve. When I was a junior staff member at the Menninger Clinic in the early 40s, my turn came to present at one of our regular staff meetings. I was assigned the task of reviewing Grinker and Spiegel's *War Neuroses in North Africa*, which details their vivid experiences with the traumatic neuroses of war and their treatment, often by abreaction under sodium pentothal. When I finished, the late Karl Menninger, who ran those meetings, declared with an acerbity that was not entirely uncharacteristic of him, "Merton, I have never known anyone else with your capacity to make something intrinsically so lively and exciting so dull and boring." Of course he was right, and I have been struggling against that propensity ever since. I hope the reader will feel I have made some progress.

So, back to the book. I began to rewrite in a more sprightly fashion, even including an anecdote from my professional life here and there, like the one about me and Dr. Karl. We called him that because there was also Dr. Will. But I still had not decided on my two audiences. The beginner should know something about the metapsychological points of view, for example, even though I essentially reject them, at least in their classical Freudian guise. But their recital would bore someone experienced in the field. How could I make the metapsychological points of view sprightly? If I could thunder them with Rapaportian excitement, that might have been interesting to a live audience, but on paper . . .

So I considered various other possibilities. Why not two books, one for the experienced and one for the beginner? But I wanted to set forth my views on the controversies for both audiences. It was not really two separate books I had in mind. I considered writing the book largely from the point of view of the experienced clinician but putting various sections, like the metapsychological points of view and the defense mechanisms, in appendices for the beginner. But that would make a big book. Years ago, when I told someone of my plan to write a textbook, he said, "For God's sake, keep it short, if you want anyone to read it."

As I reviewed various drafts, I found that one was written as though for a beginner and another for experienced therapists. My overriding interest for some years has been in technique in the context of general theory. So I decided on two books. One for the experienced and indeed essentially on technique in the context of general theory. The other would be an introductory text, including what is already familiar ground for the experienced, and therefore not in the first book, but taking up the same issues of technique, albeit in less detail. There would be overlap, of course, especially because of a common central theme of both books.

The reason for the commonality between the two books is, as will become evident to the reader, that I believe that the classical analytic

situation, with frequent sessions and couch, and the situation con-
fronting a resident doing his first case of psychological therapy should
each aim to promote something similar, which I call the "psychoanalytic situation." I believe that situation should be the goal in both
psychoanalysis proper—that is, with the standard extrinsic criteria of
couch, frequent sessions, duration, and the like—and in a psychological therapy that employs analytic technique but with different extrinsic dimensions, like sitting up, lesser frequency, shorter duration,
and the like. I will later discuss in detail the difference between this
latter kind of therapy and what is usually called dynamic psychotherapy, or psychoanalytic psychotherapy, or psychoanalytically oriented
psychotherapy. I considered symbolizing the kind of therapy I am
describing by writing it as "psycho-analytic therapy" with a hyphen,
but I concluded that the hyphen was too gimmicky and wouldn't
catch on anyhow. I considered using the term psychoanalytic therapy,
but I was afraid that it would be understood to be the kind of therapy
that Franz Alexander described under that term. But that was so long
ago that I decided I could give the term a new meaning. Although the
term psychoanalytic psychotherapy is usually used in contrast to
psychoanalysis, I mean by psychoanalytic therapy something different
from what is usually called psychoanalytic psychotherapy.

Of course, the much discussed issue of the difference between
psychoanalysis and psychotherapy is involved. In my detailed discussion I will give my rationale for including psychoanalysis with and
without the usual extrinsic criteria of psychoanalysis proper under the
broad heading psychoanalytic therapy, which aims to develop a
"psychoanalytic situation." One more word about terminology. "Psychoanalytic situation" is ordinarily used in connection with psychoanalysis proper, but I am proposing that one should also aim toward it
in what I am calling psychoanalytic therapy. Some would argue that
the term psychoanalytic situation should be confined to psychoanalysis proper, because it is so entrenched and that perhaps a term like
psychoanalytic dialogue should be used instead, since dialogue is a
major aspect of a central shift I will be discussing in the understanding
of psychoanalytic therapy as well as in psychoanalysis proper. The
term psychoanalytic dialogue is, of course, the same as the new journal
Psychoanalytic Dialogues, which was founded by an offshoot of interpersonal psychoanalysts who call themselves relationists. I decided
against "dialogue" because my view of the analytic situation is broader

than relational, as I shall discuss in terms of one-person and two-person psychologies.

To keep the volumes shorter, I decided that instead of interlarding examples in the text as is usually done, I would write a third volume of examples intended for both the beginner and the experienced. I had done the same in my monographs on transference, of which this work is a continuation.

I faced another difficult problem in deciding what book to write. I have become convinced that, in addition to the matter of dialogue, another new perspective is developing in psychoanalysis, of which Irwin Hoffman is a principal architect, among others of course. He has named it social constructivism.

Hoffman (1991) has made clear that social constructivism involves two antinomies or axes, an important distinction. One is the drive-relational antinomy, and the other is the objectivist-constructivist antinomy. Both antinomies have important implications for technique.

This volume is largely confined to issues in the drive-relational antinomy, with only a brief discussion of the objectivist-constructivist antinomy. Hoffman has already discussed the latter in a number of papers (1983, 1987, 1991, 1992a, b, 1993, 1994, in press-a, b), and has a book in preparation integrating issues in the social-constructivist paradigm.

I return to the question of my two books. What do I think the reader has in hand? Although I have written a number of chapters that would be suitable for a textbook, they are not here. This is surely not a textbook. Whether I will ever carry out the plan of presenting a book with those chapters, together with some version of the present work, that might be more suitable for beginners, I don't know. Do I feel, then, that beginners cannot usefully read this book? The encomia on book jackets in our field often say that the work will be enlightening to experienced practioners and beginners alike. I confess that I feel that way about this book. It is about what interests me the most — a basic perspective on the nature of psychological therapy informed by psychoanalytic concepts.

Another word about a textbook. Surveys of psychoanalytic theory and practice often take the form of a chronological review of Freud's work. There are several reasons for this in addition to the fact that it is easier to give a chronological account than to attempt to systematize the principles in some logical order. One reason is that psychoanalysis is to a remarkable degree the work of one man, Sigmund Freud. It has been correctly said that all psychoanalytic writing has to take a stand either in agreement or in disagreement with Freud. Another reason is that psychoanalysis underwent a rich development in Freud's own hands, often apparently in response to new findings from the psychoanalytic method. This development was cited by Freud himself as evidence that psychoanalysis is an empirical discipline in contrast to, as he put it, a philosophy with a fixed and unassailable system of tenets.

A good reason for following the chronological course is that certain elements of psychoanalysis are traceable to its history and might well not maintain the prominence they have were it not for their place in that history. Even so, I am convinced that the more useful presentation is a systematic one with interwoven points about the history.

PSYCHOANALYSIS IS IN DISARRAY

Psychoanalysis seems to be in particular disarray as of this writing. While there have always been dissenting voices and even new schools, the organized center seems to be less and less a majority viewpoint. Fragmentation appears to be the order of the day, with few evidences of synthesis of opposing viewpoints.

One can take two very different attitudes toward this state of affairs. On one hand, it might be regarded as a sign of healthy ferment and an affirmation of the claim that psychoanalysis is an advancing empirical discipline rather than a fixed and entrenched system. On the other hand, it might be regarded as a sign of something basically wrong in the conceptual framework or organizational structure of psychoanalysis that portends the dissolution of its present form.

There is no question that psychoanalysis as a therapy has lost much of the prestige it once had. Whereas formerly qualification as a psychoanalyst was almost obligatory for an aspirant to the chairmanship of a department of psychiatry, now it can be a liability. There has been a progressive decline in the number of applicants for training in institutes accredited by the American Psychoanalytic Association.

The practice of psychoanalysis is seriously threatened for reasons that are plain to see. Psychoanalysis is a very expensive procedure.

Fewer and fewer people are able to afford it on their own. Third-party payers are progressively disinclined to support it. This disinclination is especially true for that class of potential analysands who are considered most suitable for the classical analytic procedure, namely, persons who are working and maintaining a reasonable adjustment in society. The difficulties that lead such people to seek psychological help are being progressively defined as some form of difficulty in living (Sullivan) rather than as a medical disorder that warrants support by insurance written for disease and, even more questionably, by insurance under government auspices. There is disagreement among analysts as to how much an analysis is interfered with when the fee is paid by insurance in whole or in part.

At the same time, the position of psychoanalysis as therapy for psychological distress is progressively threatened by competition from other varieties of practitioners. While some psychologists practice psychoanalysis, most clinical psychologists practice competing kinds of therapy. The distinction between clinical psychologists and their colleagues in other branches of psychology has long been present. But it was not so long ago that the clinical psychologist was relegated to serve as an aide to psychiatrists, giving psychological tests for diagnostic purposes, and perhaps doing psychotherapy under supervision. Now the clinical psychologist has assumed a much more independent role, primarily as a therapist. I do not know the relative numbers of those who practice "psychoanalytic psychotherapy" and those who practice some form of behavioral, cognitive, or other nonanalytic psychotherapy.

The relationships between psychiatry, psychoanalysis, and psychology are undergoing major changes. With the phenomenal growth—and findings—of biological studies of the brain and psychopharmacology, psychiatry is swinging toward medicine and away from psychology. The primary concern of psychiatry is with the psychoses, but inevitably the lesser disorders with psychological symptomatology (I express myself in terms of symptoms to avoid a position on the relative roles of organic and psychological factors in the etiology of the psychoses) are also being viewed as physical and are treated with drugs by many psychiatrists. I refer specifically to anxiety and depression in people who are continuing to function in their social roles and show no signs of a break with reality.

Psychoanalysts are caught in the middle between psychiatrists and clinical psychologists. This is especially true in America, both North and South, where the medical identity of psychoanalysis is a good deal stronger than in Europe, though less so in South than in North America. The preponderant organized psychoanalytic group in the United States has long refused to accept non-M.D.s for training as practitioners, although for some years a few non-M.D.s planning research careers were accepted for training by the primarily medical institutes. Recently, as a result of a suit brought against medical psychoanalysts for restraint of trade, non-M.D.s with an advanced degree were for the first time in the United States deemed acceptable for training as practitioners in the medical institutes. Until recently non-M.D.s, whether planning research or practice careers, had to be passed by a central committee of the national organization, but that is no longer true, just as such approval is not required for M.D. applicants. It has also become possible for North American institutes not affiliated with the American Psychoanalytic Association to become members of the International Psychoanalytical Association.

Psychologists have long had a limited number of psychoanalytic training institutes of their own that have always accepted physicians and psychologists on an equal basis. So medical psychoanalysts, with an already shrinking clientele, now have added anxiety about lay competition to their previous objections in principle to training non-M.D.s as psychoanalytic practitioners.

The move to define psychoanalysis as a nonmedical treatment for nonmedical disorders, with a concomitant denial of claims by third-party payers, has pushed medical psychoanalysts to justify their claim to be practicing medicine by strengthening their ties with psychiatrists. To admit that non-M.D.s can practice psychoanalysis clearly weakens the claim of medical psychoanalysts to be practicing medicine.

What is happening to the practice of psychoanalysis under these conditions? Despite the qualifications of those psychoanalysts who are physicians and psychiatrists, their primary interest and expertise is in the psychological treatment of psychological disorders. They are therefore doing psychotherapy to fill the time left empty because of the dearth of analysands.

For that reason the question of the relationship between psychoanalysis and psychotherapy as special techniques is becoming even more pressing. The prevailing opinion is that they are two quite distinct techniques that it is important to keep separate, especially because analysts are considered to be always in danger of succumbing to the infiltration of psychoanalytic technique by psychotherapeutic "contaminants." Lipton quipped that a primary aim of some contemporary psychoanalytic technique seems to be to prevent a therapy from being subject to the accusation that it is "merely" psychotherapy.

It has long been felt that for one to become a good analyst a full-time analytic practice for some time is necessary. Freud said that the practice of psychoanalysis is not like a pair of spectacles that can be put on and taken off. But current graduates of training institutes must have a mixed psychoanalytic-psychotherapeutic practice. On one hand, they face the danger of the "contamination" of their psychoanalysis by psychotherapy and, on the other hand, the danger of damaging their psychotherapy by the relatively withdrawn posture still widely considered appropriate for psychoanalysis. In the latter case, they may be said to be attempting to make up for not having enough analysis in their practice by inappropriately practicing analysis on their psychotherapy patients; in the former case, they may be said to be contaminating their analytic work with psychotherapeutic techniques. I have already given my own view that this dilemma arises from the mistaken conception that analytic technique—as against psychoanalysis proper—can be practiced only with a minimum of three or four sessions a week, with the use of the couch, and with relatively less sick patients.

There are additional factors that help to account for what I have called the contemporary disarray of psychoanalysis. One is that with the recent death of Anna Freud the last personal link to the founding father has been broken. It must be remembered, however, that Freud (1926) himself was unequivocal in his support of "lay" analysts as being on a par with medical analysts.

Another factor militating against the practice of psychoanalysis is the growing disillusionment with the results of psychoanalysis as a therapy. Data are hard to come by, and analysts often object to follow-up studies because such studies require what is considered an intrusion into the analyst–analysand relationship, but the feeling is prevalent that symptoms often persist even after long analyses. Furthermore, the other therapists to whom I referred often promise much quicker and easier results. These other therapists include not only nonanalytic psychologists but social workers and even pastoral counselors as well. Medical practice acts are ambiguous as to the practice of psychotherapy, and so too are licensure requirements for various kinds of psychological counseling. Almost anyone can set up shop to practice some variety of psychological help.

How did psychoanalysis get into this kind of fix? There are various peculiarities about psychoanalysis as a discipline and its social role that I believe help us to understand how it has come about. The history of the development of psychoanalysis also provides some answers to this question. It is not the question I address in this work.

My attempt here is to present my perspective on the psychoanalytic situation as well as my views on some basic questions in psychoanalytic theory.

1

Constructivism and Hermeneutics

Before proceeding to the psychoanalytic situation as such, I want to provide the context within which I will discuss it. That context is in terms of constructivism and hermeneutics. For some time I struggled with the question of whether constructivism and hermeneutics were on the same level of abstraction or whether one was superordinate to the other. It now seems preferable to me to consider constructivism superordinate to hermeneutics, and I will try to explain why.

CONSTRUCTIVISM

Since I am not sophisticated in epistemology or philosophy, I believe it is important to state that I am using concepts like constructivism, hermeneutics, and objectivism, which have generated great bodies of controversial literature, only in a global, connotative, more or less commonsensical way.

Constructivism is the proposition that all human perception and thinking is a construction rather than a direct reflection of external reality as such. That is to say, any percept or idea is in part a function of the perceiver or thinker. Otherwise stated, any perception or idea is from the particular perspective of the perceiver or thinker. Constructivism can also be called perspectivism or relativism. Another familiar way of conveying the constructivist premise is to say that there are no facts as such. In a vivid metaphor, facts are soaked in theory.

Science—obviously based on perception and thought—is constructivist. While this may appear more obviously true for the human sciences, it is true for the natural sciences too. The natural sciences are developed by human beings. As such, they are determined in part by the nature of the perceiving or thinking human beings. They are

1

constructed from the human perspective. They are relative to that perspective.

I understand *radical* constructivism to mean questioning the certainty that there is any external reality at all or that one can know anything about external reality. I do not mean that kind of constructivism. I mean that what we understand of reality is not reality as such but the construction we make of reality. A construction is subject to the constraints of reality even if we cannot say what the reality really is. It seems like a conundrum to say that we must take account of the constraints of reality when we cannot say what reality is. Constructivism in psychoanalysis is sometimes misunderstood to mean that the analyst cannot feel sure of anything. That is not so. It is, rather, that the analyst should not function with the idea, for example, that he is dealing with unquestionable facts as to what human nature universally is. In his everyday work, the analyst is a pragmatic constructivist (Berger, 1985; Schafer, 1992). He may work with confidence, but he never abandons the perspective that he may be mistaken. Of course, the more inferential a conclusion he has reached, the more ready he is to entertain other views. This is especially true if he is dealing with another person's subjective state. Nor can one say that another person is the final arbiter of his own subjective state. That may be true for his conscious state, but psychoanalysis has discovered unconscious mentation.

HERMENEUTICS

There is a large body of philosophical studies about the nature of human knowledge generally and, within the philosophy of science, about the meaning of hermeneutics more particularly. I know that literature only second and even third hand. I know that some of that literature claims that there can be no such thing as a hermeneutic science, but that view seems to be based on the assumption that there can be a nonconstructivist science, that is, a science in which one can reach a positive, unequivocal, and certain knowledge of external reality. The model for such alleged knowledge has long been the natural sciences, but my understanding is that the natural sciences are constructivist too, even if less obviously so than matters psychological.

What then is hermeneutics? It means interpretation. How then does it differ from constructivism, since constructivism also implies interpretation, there being no such thing as a perception that is not already an interpretation? The answer is that, at least as far as psychoanalysis is concerned, hermeneutics means an interpretation of human meanings. I have difficulty defining a human meaning but, as a supreme court justice said about pornography, he could not define it but he could tell it when he saw it. I can tell it when I see it. I can offer only a global statement of what I mean by a human meaning. I mean one that includes an affective personal meaning or, more generally, psychic reality in contrast to material reality. Human meaning is really the same concept Kohut (1959) used when he wrote his famous paper on introspection and empathy. He argued that if empathy—that is, a potential capacity to feel what another human being feels—is not part of an observation, that observation is not a psychoanalytic one. I meant the same thing when I wrote that "metapsychology is not psychology" (Gill, 1976). Freudian metapsychology is not hermeneutic. Despite Freud's insistence that his metapsychology was an intrinsic aspect of psychoanalysis, he in effect defined a "psychical act" as hermeneutic. He wrote:

> Anything that is observable in mental life may occasionally be described as a mental phenomenon. The question will then be whether the particular mental phenomenon has arisen immediately from somatic, organic and material influences—in which case its investigation will not be part of psychology—or whether it is derived in the first instance from other mental processes, somewhere behind which the series of organic influences begin. It is this latter situation that we have in view when we describe a phenomenon as a mental process, and for that reason it is more expedient to clothe our assertion in the form: "the phenomenon has a sense." By "sense" we understand "meaning," "intention," "purpose" and "position in a continuous psychical context" [Freud, 1916, pp. 60–61].

Although Freud seldom used the word empathy [Einfülung], he did write this: "A path leads from identification by way of imitation to empathy, that is, to the comprehension of the mechanism by means of which we are enabled *to take up any attitude at all towards another mental life*" (Freud, 1921, p. 110n, italics added).[1]

---

[1] Professor G. W. Pigman III called my attention to a number of other appearances in Freud of the term *Einfühlung*, including one in one of the technique papers, this one not translated as empathy by Strachey.

When I say that hermeneutics involves interpretation, I recognize that the word interpretation is very broadly used. In the realm of material reality, I can "interpret" the meaning of a chemical experiment, but such an interpretation is not hermeneutic. I can interpret the Song of Songs, for all its sensuous imagery, to refer to man's relations to God. The latter interpretation is hermeneutic, even though it need not be the meaning that the Song of Songs has for everyone. By a hermeneutic meaning, I mean, for example, that a patient's bitter tirade may signify his denial that he is falling in love.

The idea of hermeneutics originally described the interpretation of religious texts. It spread to include other texts, such as those of literature, so that literary criticism is now called a hermeneutic discipline. Even a human being can be considered a text (Gergen, 1985). A crucial difference between a literary text and the human being as a text in the psychotherapeutic situation is that the human text answers back. The psychotherapeutic interpretation is met by a response; a poem does not reply to an interpretation of its meaning. It is a fixed text. I think it is a mistake to argue that the text is not fixed because it has different meanings to different readers. A new reader can come along to read the original text, except, of course, as he has been influenced by others' prior readings.

CAN THERE BE A CONSTRUCTIVIST AND A HERMENEUTIC SCIENCE?

For some time, there has been a furor in psychoanalysis as to whether psychoanalysis is a natural science or a hermeneutic discipline. The very phrase hermeneutic science has been considered by many to be an oxymoron, a self-contradiction; and constructivism is by many regarded as incapable of being scientific, since it allows for the validity of differing views of the same phenomenon.

What does it mean to say that the same phenomenon is being described? It means that there are facts in the material realm as well as events on which we can unequivocally agree. If I raise my eyebrows, we can all agree that this phenomenon took place. If a patient tells us his parents were divorced, that is a fact on which we can agree. It is not hermeneutics. One might say that the fact of the divorce is akin to material, rather than psychic, reality. But what the divorce meant to the patient is hermeneutic. We can never know it unequivocally. Freud unequivocally regarded psychoanalysis as a natural science. "What else can it be?" he asked. Those who argue that psychoanalysis is constructivist and hermeneutic are considered to be denying that psychoanalysis can be a science, because it is taken as axiomatic that there cannot be a hermeneutic or constructivist science. Indeed, the charge frequently leveled against those who consider psychoanalysis to be constructivist and hermeneutic is that this is an evasion of the responsibility of psychoanalysis to subject its theories to testing by the methods of science.

I must first point out that, while hermeneutic studies in the humanities may not be science, psychoanalysis as hermeneutics can be. As I just suggested, a poem does not reply to an interpretation, but a patient does, at least implicitly, but sometimes explicitly as well. We need not take his reply at face value, and we have a basis for continuing exploration of the validity of a meaning.

A major reason that constructivism and hermeneutics are ruled out as science is the failure to recognize that all science is constructivist, even though this is less obvious in the natural than in the humanist sciences.

An antonym to relativism is positivism. The latter assumes facts that are in no way relative to the observer. There is only one true answer. The observer can be, as it were, factored out. I will later discuss the view of the analyst as a blank screen as exemplifying the fallacy that the analyst can be factored out, that is, that his observations and interpretations are free of any contribution from his own personhood.

How can there be such a thing as science if there is no one true answer? Is science not the progressive elimination of the contribution of the observer until finally the naked, brute fact is reached? No, the contribution of the observer can never be reduced to zero. Even the statements that I raised my eyebrows and that there has been a divorce are statements in a particular context. That context can be progressively clarified by working toward its greater comprehensiveness and coherence, but the fact remains meaningful only in a context. A fact can be meaningful in a material context, but it does not become a psychoanalytic "fact" unless it is being described in a context of psychic reality. Interpretations of psychic reality can, of course, differ widely. It is a reduction to an absurdity to argue, as it often is argued, that in a constructivist-hermeneutic perspective "anything goes," or, in a current idiom for the psychotherapeutic situation, that one narrative is as good as any other or that narratives differ only in their aesthetic appeal. That kind of thinking is what I have referred to as radical constructivism.

At one time, it was believed that from the point of view of epistemology, the theory of human knowledge, a major distinction must be drawn between the natural and the human sciences, or as Dilthey (1924) put it in the German terms often used even in discussion in other languages, between the *Naturwissenschaften* and the *Geisteswissenschaften*, literally between the natural sciences and the spiritual sciences.

A major form that the argument over whether psychoanalysis is a natural or a hermeneutic science has taken is the metapsychology versus clinical, or, as I prefer, the metapsychology versus psychology (Gill, 1976) debate. I believe the issue can be formulated in the context of the preceding remark. Every discipline has a metadiscipline, that is, a context that determines the meaning of its terms. Freud's metadiscipline for psychoanalysis is his metapsychology. Freudian metapsychology is in a natural science framework; its natural scientific terms are force, energy, substance, and space. Freud's clinical theory, his psychology, is in a hermeneutic metapsychology; it deals with human meanings. Freud's metapsychology and his psychology are confusingly intertwined. A prime instance of their intertwining is Freudian drive theory, which is formulated in both natural-science and hermeneutic-science terms. Psychosexuality in Freudian theory is both energic and relational, libido and love, metapsychology and psychology. George Klein's (1976) brilliant essay on Freud's two theories of sexuality distinguishes between viewing drive theory in natural science terms or hermeneutically. Libidinous activity must be distinguished from love. Rape is also a humanly (or from another point of view, inhumanly) meaningful activity.

It is important to emphasize a point that was effectively made by Grünbaum (1984): although Freud himself did not make the distinction, his claim that psychoanalysis is a natural science is based not only on his metapsychology but on his clinical theory as well. It cannot be assumed, therefore, that Freud's belief that psychoanalysis is a natural science rests on the metapsychology alone.

As something of an aside, I insert here a remark about primary and secondary process. These concepts are constructs that certainly capture something about the nature of thought. Rejecting energic metapsychology as I do, I have been unable to accept Freud's explanation of the primary processes of displacement and condensation as resulting from the need to discharge as much psychic energy as rapidly as possible.

The most plausible alternate construction of these processes I have been able to find is Irene Fast's (1992) discussion relating them to Piaget's sensorimotor period in which meaning derives from actions, so that any constituent of the action can express the meaning of the action. In the action of sucking, for example, finger and nipple can substitute for each other; that is, meaning can be displaced from one to the other. In a condensation, the elements that are condensed can be shown to be parts of constellations that have equivalent meanings. The formulation reminds me of David Rapaport's (1951) distinction between the drive and the reality organizations of memory.

It is often said that scientific method is the same throughout the sciences. Only the subject matter differs. On the other hand, it is sometimes said— of course by those who consider that there *can* be a hermeneutic science— that the scientific method of a hermeneutic science is, or will be, different from the scientific method of the natural sciences. Just what these differences may be is a largely unexplored topic. As I said, the hermeneutic position is widely regarded as an evasion of the responsibility of psychoanalysis to test its theses for their validity; it thereby bears out the critic's claim that there cannot be such a thing as a hermeneutic "science." There are many interesting twists and turns taken by those who deal with the issues of hermeneutics in psychoanalysis. Donald Spence (1993) emphasizes the crucial need to take subjectivity (hermeneutics) into account, but he seems to do so with the idea that if one does so one will finally be able to reach brute facts. He has therefore been called a "closet positivist" by Jerome Bruner (1993), who regards the search for agreement among analysts as a mistaken enterprise. Richard Rorty (1993) takes an even more extreme position, which he calls pragmatism: "the issue about the 'scientific status' of a discipline moves away from questions about whether there are covering laws . . . and about whether these laws . . . can receive empirical confirmation . . . toward questions about whether the people who work within the discipline tend to reach consensus . . ." (p. 23).

I shrink from the task of trying to define what the scientific method is and how it may be different in the natural and in the hermeneutic sciences. Nevertheless, in the most general terms, the scientific method is the postulation of a hypothesis, the collection of data relating to that hypothesis, and the testing of that hypothesis in terms of the data according to a prescribed set of rules. Of course the rub is in how to define "data." Validation in a hermeneutic context is sometimes described as involving a "hermeneutic circle" in which the whole determines the meaning of the parts and the parts determine the meaning of the whole. The process of validation is a continuing reciprocal movement from part to whole and whole to part. Is this really any different from validation in the natural sciences? I think not, even if the circle is so much more obvious in the human sciences than in the natural sciences.

A common argument is that the natural sciences deal with causes while the human sciences deal only with reasons. But it can be cogently argued that a reason is a cause. Is making a distinction between cause and reason saying anything more than that the natural sciences deal with material reality while the hermeneutic sciences deal with psychic reality? I think not.

It is often said that hermeneutic validation rests only on comprehensiveness and consistency, while the natural sciences deal with facts. I distinguish between facts in a context of material reality and in a context of psychic reality. But, again, I argue that all science, whether natural or hermeneutic, engages in validation only in the sense that the relationships between part and whole and whole and part are made more consistent and comprehensive. Again, this says no more than that all observation and thought is meaningful only in a context or, once again, that all observation and thought is constructivist. In both the natural sciences and the hermeneutic sciences validation is subject to the constraints of reality, even though, as I said, the reality cannot be known directly. To be valid, a proposition must not contradict reality insofar as reality can be known, that is, insofar as there are observations on which we can unequivocally agree. This issue is, of course, being discussed in our literature as an opposition between a correspondence and a coherence theory of truth. Victoria Hamilton (1993), among others, has pointed out the unnecessarily sharp dichotomizing of the two as far as psychoanalytic practice is concerned. Those who insist on a correspondence theory of truth imply that they are preserving the status of psychoanalysis as a science and therefore as researchable. But where, then, is the research?

It is worth pointing out that there is a distinction between the general epistemological concept of constructivism and the specific constructivist recognition that every investigator finds his "facts" in terms of his theory, that is, in terms of the context within which he works.

Some prominent philosophers believe that psychoanalysis is a hybrid, in the words of Ricoeur (1981), a mixed "energic-semantic discourse." Habermas (1971) distinguishes between ordinary hermeneutics and psychoanalysis as a "depth hermeneutics," because psychoanalysis postulates unconscious as well as conscious psychic activity. The fact that hermeneutics is sometimes referred to as "subjectivity" has led some to the mistaken idea that hermeneutics is necessarily confined to that which is conscious. It is frequently unrecognized that there can also be a hermeneutics of non-verbal behavior.

My own view is that the concept of a mixed energic-semantic discourse is an attempt to deal with the fact that a human being is both a physical organism and a psychological person (Rubinstein, 1976). I believe that psychoanalysis can and should be a purely psychological discipline. That does not mean that I discount the role of the body in human functioning but that, at least as far as psychoanalysis is concerned, body is taken account of only in terms of its psychological significance. I will later deal with the status of the body at greater length. Here, I only want to give an example. Certainly, brain dysfunction influences human psychological functioning, but *insofar as psychoanalysis is concerned* that influence is dealt with only in the sense in which that dysfunction has personal meaning for the individual who has the dysfunction. The same brain dysfunction, that is, the same to a neurologist, may have very different personal meanings to different people. Psychoanalysis deals with the particular personal meanings.

In Ricoeur's (1981) phrase "mixed energic-semantic discourse," the term energic refers to the body, while the term semantic encompasses meaning and language. Language plays an enormously important role in psychoanalysis, and analysts like Jacques Lacan (1977) have attempted to make psychoanalysis essentially a matter of language. I believe that, important though language is, there is more than that to psychoanalysis, unless the term language is expanded beyond its ordinary meaning of a verbal system of meanings to mean any system of meanings whatsoever.

To say that psychoanalysis is hermeneutic is, therefore, to say that it is a purely psychological discipline dealing with human meanings. I like Schafer's (1983) definition, even though it can be read to say that psychoanalysis can only be a "discipline" in contrast to a "science." It reads as follows:

> What has been presented here amounts to a hermeneutic version of psychoanalysis for . . . psychoanalysis is an interpretive discipline rather than a natural science. It deals in language and equivalents of language. Interpretations are re-descriptions or retellings of action along the lines peculiar to psychoanalytic interest. . . . The facts are what the analyst makes them out to be; they are a function of the specifically psychoanalytic questions that guide this narrational project, and these questions implement the narrative strategies that are favored by the analyst's own presuppositions, however unsystematized these might be [pp. 255–256].

Rather than saying that "the facts are what the analyst makes them out to be," I prefer to say that the facts are what analyst and analysand come to agree are facts. This formulation does not imply that I see the analytic situation as symmetrical for analyst and analysand. And it is important to emphasize that the analyst's presuppositions have affective as well as intellectual sources (Hoffman, 1991, 1992a).

Many analysts are disturbed by such a definition. For one thing, they misread the connotations of "narrative." They think that means a story, with the implication that one story is as good as any other, that all that is sought is a consistent and cohesive story having no necessary relationship to what actually happened— in short, a fiction. In other words, the constraints of reality are ignored.

Nothing could be further from the truth. Such a view is an absurd distortion of the concept of constructivism and of the analyst's contribution to the analytic situation. Every analyst knows that he or she significantly contributes to an analytic situation. To be sure, the criteria of a narrative do not include a necessarily veridical correspondence to what "actually" happened, for it is axiomatic for psychoanalysis that it is not only what "actually" happened (that is, as described in external reality) which matters, but rather how what happened was experienced by the two participants, often very differently.

But within limits, which vary from situation to situation, what happened in the past and what is happening now in the analytic situation as well as outside of it, can be stated in two distinct ways: as it would appear to an external observer and how it is experienced in psychic reality. Apparently kindly parents may have been experienced as severe or even vice versa, but the relationship between behavior and how it is experienced is not random. Generalizations can be made. It is true that in any particular instance there can be an astonishing discrepancy between how behavior would be described by an external observer and how it is experienced, but then external observers of one and the same behavior can also differ among themselves as to its significance. That is what makes psychoanalysis so exquisitely individual; it is why the analysand's narrative of his past can change as an analysis progresses. The important point is that the meaning of a behavior varies with the individual concerned. Analyst and analysand may experience quite differently what goes on between them. The analyst may experience himself as friendly while the patient may experience him as anything but friendly, and, less often, the opposite may be the case.

There are additional important reasons why narratives of an event may be experienced differently. A major one for psychoanalysis is that an event may be described very differently as a function of whether it is being understood in a conscious, preconscious, or unconscious context. What is manifestly friendly may be unconsciously hostile and vice versa. The analyst may be interpreting something in terms of what he believes it means to the patient unconsciously, while the patient may understand it only in its manifest conscious context. I will later pursue the issues of how to deal with disparity of experience and understandings between analyst and analysand as well as the role of the analyst as expert.

Another way of understanding variant readings of an event is in terms of Freud's concept of overdetermination, perhaps better conceived of as multiple determination in line with Robert Waelder's (1930) concept of multiple function. Any behavior, Waelder argued, must simultaneously satisfy the requirements of id, ego, superego, reality, and consistency within the ego itself. A view of behavior from only one of these aspects is a partial one, and partial views will differ. And if two people are viewing an event from different partial angles, again, there will be different narratives. The analyst, for example, commonly sees a behavior as defensive while to the patient it may be adaptive. Of course, a behavior can be both defensive and adaptive; but the patient experiences the defense as enabling an adaptive equilibrium, whereas the analyst sees it as maladaptive from the point of view of his goal for the analysis.

So I conclude that psychoanalysis is constructivist and hermeneutic and that it can still be a science. The reason I was puzzled as to the superordinacy of constructivism or hermeneutics is that I did not realize that interpretation in the natural sciences is not the same as interpretation in the human sciences. Since all sciences are constructivist, while only the human sciences are hermeneutic, I make constructivism superordinate to hermeneutics.

An important way in which the concept of constructivism has been misunderstood is that an antinomy is set up between constructivism and discovery; that is, that nothing can be uncovered in the analytic process that has been there but not known, waiting to be found out, so to speak. There is no doubt that during the analytic process, memories, not only of events but also of feelings about these events at the time, can be recovered. Even so, the context in which these memories are recovered and the changed meanings that may now be ascribed to them make these recoveries constructions rather than simple uncoverings.

I realize that I have essentially stated my own opinion on matters that have been and will continue to be the subject of serious debate. I want to add only that I am convinced that there are and will be more methods by which to decide between the relative merits of competing propositions both as to psychic development and the technique of therapy.

With these remarks, I have now prepared the ground for a more specific discussion of the psychoanalytic situation, to which I turn. In what follows, I will occasionally introduce a term or concept that I will deal with in detail only later on. My justification is that no reader is likely to come to this book entirely ignorant of the subject. It would be tedious and break continuity to try to make the sequence of presentation such that any new term is dealt with in detail at once. I have not attempted to review the literature comprehensively on any topic with which I deal except perhaps free association. I cite only those contributions that come to mind as I write. Because this book was composed piecemeal over a fairly long period of time there are overlaps and repetitions here and there, especially of certain basic ideas. I have not attempted to expunge them, not merely to avoid the labor involved but more because I believe they contribute to the clarity of presentation.

The amount of space I have devoted to any particular issue is not necessarily an indication of how important I consider it to be but rather of whether I feel I have something useful to say about it.

2

The Internal and the External

Before I take up the psychoanalytic situation, I will discuss more specifically a very general issue in psychic functioning, namely, the relationship between internal and external factors.

What is probably the single most fateful event in the history of psychoanalysis is Freud's discovery that he had been mistaken in believing that most of the tales of childhood sexual seduction that his patients told him in the 1890s had actually taken place. When his earlier conclusion fell of its own improbable weight, he was crestfallen. But he was able to snatch an important victory from the jaws of defeat. The tales, he concluded, were for the most part fantasies, not descriptions of external events that had actually taken place. He further concluded that such fantasies were the expression of universally present, innate, instinctual drives.

What took place was a massive swing from an emphasis on external factors to internal ones. The battle between the relative importance of external and internal became a central theme of psychoanalytic theory and practice and continues to the present. I use the very general terms internal and external because at first I want to be nonspecific and use terms as general as possible. I will soon turn to the many more specific pairs in which the internal–external dichotomy is expressed.

I think it will be clarifying to say at the outset that no one really believes that any significant human behavior is due solely to either internal or external factors. Although Freud did come perilously close at times to opting for internal factors alone (e.g., that the "primal fantasies" are phylogenetically determined or that shame about sexuality appears spontaneously), what are often expressed as dichotomies are actually matters of emphasis and hierarchy, not a denial that the other exists and even is very important. Although the dichotomy is often expressed as though only one or the other matters, it is the

15

relative emphases on internal and external that are what the dispute is all about.

It is equally important to make clear that to speak of internal and external factors as though they were a simple dichotomy is false. In human psychological functioning the external world is significantly constructed by the internal world, and the internal world is significantly constructed by the external world. In short, we deal with a mutually interactive constructivist circle. I am taking the position that the dichotomy, in the sense of simple independent entities, is epistemologically untenable.

SUBJECT AND OBJECT

With the development of the constructivist point of view, the concept of the relationship between subject and object has changed. Formerly regarded as dichotomous, each is now seen as shaping the other; each, that is, is an integration of itself and the other. Yet there is also a sense in which each retains its independence.

Self psychology has a curious position on this issue as seen in the concept of the selfobject. Among self psychologists, Arnold Goldberg (1990) has been the most explicit about how the concept of the selfobject — written as one word — breaks down the dichotomy between subject and object. The selfobject is said to be part of the self, indeed even to be constitutive of the self. That carries the idea too far, even if only for an archaic selfobject, because it implies that the object has no independent existence, being only what the subject makes of it to realize its own purposes. In reference to an archaic selfobject, as Kohut puts it, the self feels that it is related to the selfobject as to one of its own limbs. I find this a solipsistic position in which the selfobject has no attributes of its own. Otherwise stated, the reality of the object is considered to impose no constraints on what the self makes of it.

The self-psychological literature holds that the situation changes with maturation so that the object becomes an independent center of initiative; that is, it has some independence as well. But that does not mean that self and object become dichotomous. The self continues to construe, that is, to construct, the object to a greater or lesser degree according to its needs. Even though some self psychologists even speak of adversarial selfobjects (Wolf, 1988), it is still an adversarial selfobject, not an adversarial object. As Kohut (1977) argues, and here I agree, the self requires selfobjects throughout life. This view contradicts the classical belief that the goal of development should be toward ever greater, if not complete, autonomy.

One of the flaws in self psychology is that it fails to make the reciprocal point about the object, although there are some discussions in self psychology that recognize that the self can be a selfobject to the object.

What is missing is what might be called an objectself, again written as one word. One could say that, from the point of view of the self, the object is a selfobject while the self is an objectself. I realize that the terminology is awkward, but it makes the point.

In classical analysis, subject and object remain dichotomous. The subject construes the object, but if the analyst differs with the analysand about how an object is to be construed, the analysand's construal tends to be regarded as a distortion. It is recognized that sometimes it is the analyst who is mistaken if he differs with the analysand, but the analyst's miscontrual then tends to be regarded as an unfortunate countertransferential departure from objectivity.

Goldberg (1990) is of the opinion that only self psychology has overcome the dichotomy of subject and object in its concept of selfobject. While it is true that the dichotomy persists in classical analysis, the constructivist position overcomes it for both subject and object. It has the virtue of applying the same concept to subject and object and of recognizing the constraints, or, more generally, the influences, that each exerts on the other, along with the sense in which each has an independent existence as well.

The constructivist position, at least in the hands of Hoffman (1991), retains the terms subject and object instead of using the new term selfobject (and what I have argued is its implicit correlate, the objectself). The retention of the old terms, of course, invites the misunderstanding that the old dichotomy has been maintained, but the new self-psychological terms have the disadvantage of obscuring the sense in which the subject and object are independent.

I too decided to retain the old term in my work on transference, but I redefined transference and countertransference as being contributed to by both participants and shaped by one another. I now see that transference and countertransference and their relationship are specific instances of the relationship between self and object and between internal and external.

The constraints imposed by the internal are what is constitutionally given as well as what has become internalized. The constraints imposed by the external influence our experience of reality, which we cannot know directly but whose influence nevertheless imposes constraints.

It is useful to ask what the relationship is between the classical concept of narcissistic transference and the self-psychological concept of selfobject transference. The difference lies not in the isolated phenomenon but in how it is evaluated. In classical analysis, narcissistic transference is the "selfish" use of the object for the self's own purposes with a disregard of the needs of the other. The goal of development is correspondingly toward autonomy and mutuality. In self psychology the narcissistic transference is a part of normal development and remains a lifelong necessity. The difference is something like an illegitimate wish versus a normal need. Goldberg (personal communication) believes that the difference is so great that to regard narcissistic and selfobject transferences as alternate terms can only be grossly misleading. Of course, there are pathological narcissistic and selfobject needs too.

To the extent that Kleinian theory sees the infant's construal of the parental object as determined solely by the infant's fantasies and unrelated to the qualities of the object, the self is no less solipsistic than the archaic selfobject of self psychology, although the Kleinian and self psychology pictures of the infant are very different. British object relations theory primarily dichotomizes self and object despite some recognition of an intrinsic relation between the two as, for example, in Winnicott's statement that there cannot be a baby or a mother but only a baby and a mother couple. The relational school, as exemplified by the work of Mitchell (1993), is constructivist and thus sees subject and object as shaping each other. Other relationalists do not necessarily follow him in this regard. The concept of intersubjectivity advanced by Stolorow, Brandchaft, and Atwood (1987) offers another constructivist view of subject and object; in this way intersubjectivists depart from mainstream self psychology.

INTERNAL AND EXTERNAL

In what follows, I speak of internal and external factors, but it is always to be assumed that each is also a function of the other.

The classical Freudian position emphasizes the internal factor, which is understood to be dichotomously separate from the external factor. Yet it was Freud himself who proposed a concept and name for the joint functioning of internal and external. In "Types of Onset of Neurosis," Freud (1912a) wrote: "Psychoanalysis has warned us that we must give up the unfruitful contrast between external and internal factors, between experience and constitution, and has taught us that we shall invariably find the cause of the onset of neurotic illness in a particular psychical situation which can be brought about in a variety of ways" (p. 238). The term Freud devised to overcome the "unfruitful contrast" was "complemental series." Although he does not actually use this term in the following quotation, he clearly speaks to the importance of the concept. The passage is further noteworthy because, ironically, Freud (1912b) defends himself against the charge of overlooking the internal factor, whereas the more usual charge is that he overlooks, or at least underplays, the external factor.

> It must be understood that each individual, through the combined operation of his innate disposition and the influences brought to bear on him during his early years, has acquired a specific method of his own in his conduct of his erotic life—that is, in the pre-conditions to falling in love which he lays down, in the instincts he satisfies and the aims he sets himself in the course of it [p. 99].

And to this, he adds the following footnote:

> I take this opportunity of defending myself against the mistaken charge of having denied the importance of innate (constitutional) factors because I have stressed that of infantile impressions. A charge such as this arises from the restricted nature of what men look for in the field of causation: in contrast to what ordinarily holds good in the real world, people prefer to be satisfied with a single causative factor. Psychoanalysis has talked a lot about the accidental factors in etiology and little about the constitutional ones; but that is only because it was able to contribute something fresh to the former, while, to begin with, it knew no more than was commonly known of the latter [p. 99n].

Is Freud implying that with the study of instinctual drive psychoanalysis came to know a good deal more about "constitutional" factors?

We refuse to posit any contrast in principle between the two sets of etiological factors; on the contrary, we assume that the two sets regularly act jointly in bringing about the observed result. Endowment and Chance [also in Greek in the original] determine a man's fate — rarely or never one of these powers alone. The amount of etiological effectiveness to be attributed to each of them can only be arrived at in every individual case separately. These cases may be arranged in a series according to the varying proportion in which the two factors are present, and this series will no doubt have its extreme cases. We shall estimate the share taken by constitution or experience differently in individual cases according to the stage reached by our knowledge; and we shall retain the right to modify our judgment along with changes in our understanding. Incidentally, one might venture to regard constitution itself as a precipitate from the accidental effects produced on the endlessly long chain of our ancestors [p. 99n].

The last remark is an expression of Freud's Lamarckism, a position to which he steadfastly held,[2] with reference, for instance, to primal fantasies. Freud said, for example, that if a child had no experiences that would account for castration anxiety, the child would have such anxiety anyhow by virtue of heredity. But I must again emphasize that Freud conceived of constitution (internal) and accidental (external) factors as dichotomous. In his last important paper "Analysis Terminable and Interminable," Freud (1937a) expressed prognosis in terms consistent with his model of a complemental series: analysis has its best results when the major issue in pathology is traumatic rather than constitutional.

Nevertheless, Freud's own vacillation as to the relative importance of internal and external may be seen in these remarkable passages from the end of the account of the Wolf Man. I cite them in full because they are not commonly noted and because they are contrary to the widely held belief that Freud was so firmly an "intrapsychist," that is, he believed that the primary emphasis falls on the innate. First he states the essentially innate view:

---

[2]Laplanche (1987) suggests that Freud was not really a Lamarckian because Lamarckian inherited characteristics are adaptive, while Freud's are not. When I mentioned this to Frank Sulloway, he said that, in fact, some "Lamarckian" characteristics are nonadaptive. Slavin and Kriegman (1992) point out Freud did not accept the objectionable aspect of Lamarckism — teleology.

Whenever experiences fail to fit in with the hereditary schema, they become remodeled in the imagination. . . . It is precisely such cases that are calculated to convince us of the independent existence of the schema. We are often able to see the schema triumphing over the experience of the individual, as when in our present case a boy's father became a castrator and a menace of his infantile sexuality in spite of what was in other respects an inverted Oedipus complex. . . . the contradictions between experience and the schema seem to supply the conflicts of childhood with an abundance of material.

The second problem is not far removed from the first, but it is incomparably more important. If one considers the behavior of the four-year old child towards the re-activated primal scene or even if one thinks of the far simpler reactions of the one-and-one-half year old child when the scene was actually experienced, it is hard to dismiss the view that some sort of hardly definable knowledge, something, as it were, preparatory to an understanding, was at work in the child at the time [Freud, 1918, pp. 119–120].

The formulation seems strikingly like the Kleinian view of primitive fantasy, albeit much less elaborated in specifics.

Now comes a footnote that seems to cast doubt on the whole matter: "I must once more emphasize the fact that these reflections would be vain if the dream and the neurosis had not themselves occurred in infancy" (p. 120).

The main text continues:

We can form no conception of what this may have consisted in; we have nothing at our disposal. The single analogy—and it is an excellent one—of the far-reaching instinctive [here is a footnote by Strachey who says that the German here is indeed *instinktiv* and not *triebhaft*, the latter being regularly translated "instinctual"] knowledge of animals.

If human beings do possess an instinctive endowment such as this, it would not be surprising that it should be very particularly concerned with the process of sexual life, even though it could not be by any means confined to them. [Note the important statement that the innate cannot be only sexual.] This instinctive factor would then be the nucleus of the unconscious, a primitive kind of mental activity, which would later be dethroned and overlaid by human reason, when that faculty came to be acquired, but which in some people, perhaps in everyone, would retain the power of drawing down to it the higher mental processes. [Note the important implication that there is no innate relation to reality, in contrast to Freud's late speculation of an innate ego.] Repression would be the return to this instinctive stage, and man would thus be paying for his great new acquisition with his liability to neurosis, and would be bearing witness by the possibility of the neuroses to the existence of these earlier, instinctive-like preliminary stages. The significance of the traumas of early childhood would lie in their contributing material to this unconscious which would save it from being worn away by the subsequent course of development [p. 120].

I find the idea that the innate schema can be worn away by experience startling in the light of Freud's emphasis on the universality and centrality of the innate. Is this again Lamarckism? Furthermore, the idea that trauma can contribute to the innate unconscious seems to blur the usual classical distinction between the innate and the experiential. Could this be a hint of a constructivist position on the innate and the experiential? The text continues with a virtual about-face:

I am aware that the expression has been given in many quarters to thoughts like these, which emphasize the hereditary, phylogenetically acquired factor in human life. In fact, I am of the opinion that people have been far too ready to find room for them and ascribe importance to them in psychoanalysis [!]. I consider that they are only admissible when psychoanalysis strictly observes the correct order of precedence, and, after forcing its way through the strata of what has been acquired by the individual, comes at last upon traces of what has been inherited [p. 121].

So here we find Freud, the champion of the innate, insisting that the innate should be considered seriously only after an exhaustive effort to account for a phenomenon by experience. In Haeckel's terms, this would translate as ontogeny taking precedence over phylogeny, in matters of technique at least.

Here are some of the ways that the distinction between internal and external is expressed: constitution versus experience (as described earlier); innate versus experiential; drive versus (object) relational; intrapsychic versus interpersonal; fantasy versus perception; psychic reality versus material reality; inner world versus outer world; asocial versus social.

In many but not all of these pairs, the internal factor is instinctual drive (presumably innate) and fantasy, whereas the external factor is interpersonal, that is, something involving object relations. In psychoanalytic theory, interpersonal theory and object relations theory are not synonymous, as I will later discuss. But let us first consider the dichotomy of drive and object relations.

The difference of opinion begins with the very beginning of life. Is the infant primarily related to its caretakers, or is such a relationship secondary to gratification of bodily needs? Note again that it is not a matter of either/or but rather of primary or secondary.

The obvious primary bodily need is for food. Is the relationship with the mother secondary to her provision of food? A famous experiment by Harlow (1958) tested the alternatives by providing infant monkeys with two artificial "mothers"—a wire frame monkey with food and a terry-cloth monkey without food. The monkeys, of course, periodically went to the food monkey when they were hungry, but it was the terry-cloth "mother" on which they spent most of their time and to which they went when they were frightened. They were responding to the feel of the terry cloth as to a mother monkey. But that still leaves the question of whether they were responding to the "mother" secondarily to the feel of the terry cloth. Does the infant respond to the mother "as such" without such responsiveness being grounded in some sensory modality? Or is this very question nonsensical, since there must always be some connection, internal or external, to sustain such a response.

And what of the infant's smile? The infant smiles at first at any human face but soon in particular at the mothering person. I am not very familiar with the extensive and fascinating recent research on the relationship between mother and infant (see Lichtenberg, 1983), but I have the impression that there is much evidence that the infant relates to the outside world from the very beginning; hence Freud's concept of a primary autistic phase is untenable.

One way Freud expressed the idea that the interpersonal relationship is secondary to the drive was by saying that the most variable aspect of a drive is its object. But he also expressed the opinion that a drive may become unalterably fixed to a particular object, such fixation representing a pathological loss of normal plasticity. Although strong and enduring object relationships are normal, it is nevertheless pathological to be unable to seek a new object to replace a lost one. Another striking way in which the secondary status of the relation to reality is expressed is Freud's (1915) assertion that the initial attitude of a person to the outside world is hate. Since external reality involves an unavoidable influx of stimuli, it follows, according to Freud's metapsychological energic postulates, that an organism responds primarily to the influx of stimuli from the outside as energy to be gotten rid of. In this sense, the primary relationship to the outside world is one of hate. Initially at least, reality is regarded as a hindrance to what would otherwise be the rapid discharge of energy.

I noted that though the pairs—inner-outer, internal-external, drive-object relations— are dichotomously stated, the controversy is actually a matter of emphasis or hierarchy. Let us briefly consider those theories in which emphasis and superordinacy rest with the external factor.

Such a model is often mistakenly taken to be an essentially environmentalist one, that is, a model that allegedly sees the mind as a blank slate that is written on by experience. From the point of view of classical Freudian theory, such a *tabula rasa* conception is basically wrong, because it omits the individual's own contribution (the internal factor) to his experience. Such a conception is derided by classical theorists as superficial and naively optimistic because it seems to imply that with a favorable environment there need be no conflict and no psychopathology. It is allegedly a theory that absolves the patient of any responsibility for his troubles and strengthens his tendency to blame others. It would thus undermine any therapeutic program designed to motivate a patient to help himself.

A *purely* environmentalist theory would indeed deserve such criticism, but it is not true that a "relational structure" model (Greenberg and Mitchell, 1983) need be so purely environmentalist. What is true is that the shift of emphasis toward the environment in the relational model theory as compared with drive theory, as well as the failure of many relational model theorists to pay much attention to innate factors, makes *some* relational model theories seem to be purely environmental ones. Recent books by Mitchell (1993) and Greenberg (1991) are the best statements to date by relational model theorists that attempt to take account of the internal factors as well. It nonetheless remains true that even those theorists subordinate internal factors (Slavin and Kriegman, 1992), surely as compared with the classical model. Harry Stack Sullivan (1940, 1953) is sometimes misunderstood as denying internal factors altogether. Actually, he did not, but he did regard all psychic activity as taking place in an interpersonal context, and he occasionally seemed to deny the existence of a self apart from such a context (Sullivan, 1964). While interpersonalists do take some account of internal factors, Levenson, a leading interpersonalist, leaves them as a vague product of "imagination" (see Gill, 1993).

While in a drive model the internal factor is superordinate, various drive-model theorists attribute varying significance to external factors. In the following passage, Freud (1921), the original exponent of the drive model, most clearly emphasizes the importance of the external factor: "In the individual's mental life someone else is invariably involved, as a model, as an object, as a helper, as an opponent; and so from the very first, individual psychology, in this extended but entirely justifiable sense of the words, is at the same time social psychology as well" (p. 69).

For many theorists, the Freudian drive model has become so stamped as giving preeminence to innate factors that disagreement with it is considered tantamount to rejecting the role of innate factors altogether. But a model in which interpersonal relations are superordinate, or even simply important, need not omit innate factors. Many relational theorists see the present-day classical model as inconsistent in the sense that it attributes major importance to early experience and then minimizes contemporary experience, even though it sees early experience as represented in internal schemata. Mitchell (1988) has discussed such a perspective in detail under the heading of "developmental tilt." Another model may take the role of innate factors for granted and discuss mainly interpersonal matters. An example is the separation-individuation theory espoused by Margaret Mahler (1968).

The terms intrapsychic and interpersonal have primarily connotative rather than denotative value. Intrapsychic implies that innate drives are primary, with relatively less emphasis on experience, while interpersonal implies experience as primary with relatively less emphasis on the innate. Again, each term implies a misleading caricature of the other, for the intrapsychic position also deals with interpersonal relations, while the interpersonal position also recognizes an intrapsychic world. Each term thus actually encompasses both internal and external factors. Even the term intrapsychic itself is ambiguous, since it does not stipulate whether the intrapsychic is innate or an internalization of the external or both.

Another way in which the dichotomy between internal and external may be formulated is in terms of what constitutes the basic unit for the analysis of human behavior. In the drive view it is a biological organism; in the relational view, it is a person (Gill, 1983). Kernberg (1976) straddles the fence by describing the basic unit as a self-representation, an object representation, and an affect relating the two. The sexual and aggressive drives, he proposes, arise during the course of development.

There is now increasing emphasis on interpersonal relations in the several Freudian schools, but whether implicitly or explicitly, the interpersonal perspective remains subordinate to the drive perspective. Greenberg and Mitchell (1983) have shown how the Freudian schools deal with the data relating to interpersonal relations by "accommodation" without relinquishing the basic drive perspective. A parallel movement for the "accommodation" of data relating to drive on the part of the interpersonal perspective is also present, although to a much lesser degree.

The term interpersonal often connotes an emphasis on current, here-and-now relations, while the term object relations often connotes an emphasis on intrapsychic object relations in the Kleinian school. In the British object relations school, however, there is added to intrapsychic object relations some emphasis on external object relations. Kleinian object relations theory holds that the British object relations school is too adaptively oriented in contrast to its own emphasis on innately determined object relations and vice versa. Both object relations schools consider interpersonal relations theories to downplay intrapsychic object relations and, of course, drive considerations as well. The difference is not merely a matter of emphasis but lies in what is accorded superordinacy.

An important basis for the dispute between the "intrapsychists" and the interpersonalists is that the former believe the latter to be concerned with interpersonal relations only in the manifest sense in which such relations are viewed from the outside. They therefore refer to interpersonalist theories as sociological rather than psychoanalytic (Kohut, 1971; Schwaber, 1992). Although some interpersonal theories may merit the charge, the major exponents of interpersonal theory, as represented by the faculty of the William Alanson White Institute, for example, understand interpersonal relations not in this sociological sense but as they are *experienced* in psychic reality. In this sense, particular interpersonal relations that seem equivalent to an outside observer may in fact have vastly different meanings in the psychic reality of the participants. Classical analysts often fail to recognize that most relationists and interpersonalists alike are thoroughly cognizant of the centrality of psychic reality.

I emphasize again that the concept of constructivism is different from the concept that all phenomena have both internal and external components, for in constructivism the internal plays a role in shaping the external and the external plays a role in shaping the internal. Positing a division between internal and external is misleading unless it is recognized that each contributes to shaping the other. As I mentioned, Stolorow et al. (1987) invoke the notion of an intersubjectivity, that is, an interaction between the psychic reality of two people in interaction, although Stolorow is less explicit about the role of innate internal factors.

Despite these continuing debates among proponents of different viewpoints, there is no doubt that the past decade has seen a gradual shift in the psychoanalytic world to a more equable balance between internal and external factors, with progressively greater attention paid to the external factors. As is inevitably the case, the pendulum can swing too far.

What seems to me of singular importance is to avoid adopting a general position on the relative importance of the two factors. Each case, and by case I mean the gamut from a principle to an event in a particular analysis, must be decided on its own merits. Attention to either factor can be used as a defense against the other. I believe the more common classical error is to move to the internal factor as a defense against the external rather than the reverse. I refer to a jump to the genetics of a problem or to drive issues, for example, to avoid dealing with the transference in the here-and-now or to attitudinal issues, respectively. The more common interpersonal or relational error is, of course, the reverse. Deciding where the emphasis should lie in a particular instance remains the art of psychoanalysis. A recent paper by Inderbitzin and Levy (in press) argues that while "all is grist for the mill" formerly meant that all the experiential *events* should be analyzed, it now means for many that any experiential event *can* be analyzed. The result, they feel, is often relatively unrestrained behavior by the analyst in relation to the analysand, even outside the analytic situation. They argue that therefore the experiential can be a defense against the intrapsychic. Their point is well taken, but so too can the reverse be true, that is, that the intrapsychic can be used as a defense against the experiential, especially the here-and-now interaction in the analytic situation.

As I will later discuss, one can describe the three major psychoanalytic models – drive-ego, object (including interpersonal), and self – in terms of their respective conceptual/interpretive hierarchies. Drive-ego translates self and object issues into drive-ego terms. Object psychology translates drive-ego and self issues into object terms, and self psychology translates drive-ego and object issues into self terms. But each takes account, to varying degrees, of the other two.

To summarize: I have presented a view of psychoanalysis as including both the innate and the experiential, the two shaping each other in a constructivist conceptualization. The intrapsychic includes both the innate and the internalized experiential, the latter understood as it is experienced in psychic reality. The same model has been presented by Slavin and Kriegman (1992) in the context of modern evolutionary theory. It is interesting that, like Freud, they speculate that the innate may be the precipitate of evolutionary experience. Rapaport (1957) presented a similar model in accounting for the relative autonomy of the innate and the experiential. He emphasized innate apparatuses of adaptation to external reality. Hartmann (1948) emphasized both the estrangement of the id from reality and the significance of an average expectable environment. It remains true that the great discovery peculiar to psychoanalysis, the internal factor in the sense of unconscious fantasy, is the one that psychoanalysis must zealously protect.

CONFLICT AND DEFICIT

Another form which the controversy over the relative roles of internal and external takes is evident in the relationship between the concepts of conflict and deficit. Kris (1956), in an oft-quoted statement, described psychoanalysis as psychology from the point of view of conflict.

To define psychoanalysis as psychology from the point of view of conflict might seem to make psychoanalysis a psychology of pathology rather than a general psychology. But if the nature of the human psyche is such that conflict is inevitable, healthy as well as ill people must endure conflict; so psychoanalysis remains a psychology of the normal as well as of the pathological. But that does not make psychoanalysis a general psychology except as a psychology of personality. There are aspects of psychology – the functioning of the sense organs, for example – that are outside the domain of psychoanalysis except insofar as their functioning is disturbed by conflict. Hartmann's (1948) concept of sensory and motor systems as primarily autonomous apparatuses hardly qualifies as a contribution to the normal psychology of these systems. Even though Freud wrote that in normal functioning id, ego, and superego operate in harmony, even to the point where it is difficult to distinguish one from the other, in classical psychoanalysis the innate drives are so conceived as to make conflict inevitable.

Once again, then, in classical psychoanalysis the internal is superordinate to the external. For example, the universally present Oedipus complex – often described as the central conflict of humanity – is composed of wishes that society (at least our society) condemns. But a conflict with societal norms is not yet an internal conflict. The internalization of the norms with the formation of the superego results in internal or intersystemic conflict. But there is yet a third kind of possible conflict, that between two conflicting aims, both of which are innate. There are then three kinds of possible conflict, between the innate and the external environment, between the innate and the internalized external, and between two conflicting innate aims.

The antinomy between conflict and deficit has become a much discussed issue because Kohut's self psychology is said by classical analysts to emphasize deficit over conflict and thus not to be truly psychoanalytic. Deficit as conceived of in self psychology is understood by classical analysts to result from a problem in interpersonal relations and thus to stamp self psychology as an interpersonal rather than an intrapsychic theory. For example, for Kohut's (1984) self psychology, the Oedipus complex, rather than being an inevitable source of serious conflict, can be, with the proper experience, a "joyous" phase of development, although Kohut does not deny that *some* oedipal conflict is always present. Where the emphasis is on deficit, experience is given a greater role than the innate or, more generally, the internal, in bringing about psychopathology. Indeed, self psychology holds a paradoxical position on this question of the intrapsychic and interpersonal.

Some self psychologists insist vehemently that their position is an intrapsychic one (Goldberg, 1986). I have already said that I believe one reason for this is that they do not realize that interpersonalists deal with interpersonal relationships in terms of how they are intrapsychically experienced. Some self psychologists recognize drive relations between self and object (Bacal and Newman, 1990), while others seem to recognize only the concept of "selfobject," which the subject defines in terms of whether it satisfies the self's need for mirroring, idealization, or twinning. In fact, it is a common view among classical analysts that self psychologists not only overemphasize interpersonal relationships but also interact with their patients to a degree that means they are practicing psychotherapy and not psychoanalysis, as the two terms are usually distinguished and as I described earlier.

Despite some self psychologists' minimization of the interpersonal in the theory of self psychology, self psychology paradoxically lays heavy stress on whether the analysand's history was with caretakers who responded adequately to the child's need for approval and recognition and fulfilled the child's need for a figure to look up to, even idealize. Self psychologists place this heavy emphasis not only on the child's interactional history but also on the analysand's current interaction with the analyst as well. They say that the analyst strives to be empathic but also that he inevitably will make blunders. Indeed, they regard inevitable episodes of failure to empathize correctly to be an essential ingredient of what they call "transmuting internalization," which sounds very much like mini-identification with the analyst. Surely such considerations as these emphasize the importance of the interpersonal experience of the analysand in both the past and the present.

A commonly proposed position is that conflict and deficit are two different ways of looking at the same phenomenon and that thus they are always present together. It is argued that conflict may interfere with development and therefore be responsible for the absence of something that otherwise would have developed; whereas a deficit inevitably results in a conflict, since what is missing becomes the focus of a conflict between the wish for what is missing and the repudiation of the wish. As an example in broad terms, a conflict over accepting love may lead to defense against receptivity to it (deficit) even when it is available. Of course, an integrated view would take account of both conflict and deficit, that is, of internal and external factors.[3]

The issue is thoroughly discussed in a recent monograph entitled *Conflict and Compromise* (Dowling, 1991), which should actually be entitled *Conflict and Deficit*. In it, the lone self psychologist upholder of the concept of deficit, Paul Ornstein, meets a barrage of criticism. The monograph includes clinical material too and is therefore especially worth reading. I have elsewhere (Gill, 1994b) discussed the monograph in detail.

In part, one of the reasons mainstream analysis rejects the concept of deficit is that it is espoused by self psychologists who also reject classical drive theory, so deficit is "guilt by association." Many analysts do, in fact, accept the concept of deficit, but they call it by other names, such as developmental defect.

Another important reason for the rejection of the concept of deficit is that the idea of deficit connotes to many —and it cannot be denied that it is sometimes so dealt with by some self psychologists—an absence of something, a hole in the psyche. The notion of a hole in the psyche of course makes no sense. Psychic structure may be other than desirable, but it cannot be absent.

The idea of a hole in the psyche exerts a pernicious effect on both theory and practice, because a manifest subjective sense of deficit or absence on the part of the analysand may be accepted by the analyst without further investigation. To the mainstream analyst, a manifest subjective sense of deficit is simply a point of origin for the further investigation and analysis of this sense of deficit. The point has been made a number of times in our literature. Kohut (1977) provides some basis for this criticism of self psychology in his concepts of "self-state dreams" and "empty depression," even in the concept of fragmentation. Unfortunately, these terms, certainly the last two, are sometimes not dealt with by self psychologists as metaphors, which is what they

---

[3]One of my analysts once said that if my parents' behavior accounted for 95% of my troubles and it was my experience of their behavior that accounted for the remaining 5%, it was only that 5% in which he was interested. I see his point more clearly now than I did then, but I still think I was right to become enraged.

are. So again we have the familiar charge against self psychologists: not only do they allegedly deny drive – and mainstream analysts find, of course, that the analysis of these metaphors leads to drive issues – but they allegedly accept the superficial manifest conscious instead of probing for the underlying hidden unconscious.

The implication that a deficit calls for remedial activity by the analyst, to make up for what is missing, is yet another connotation of deficit that accounts for its rejection by mainstream analysts. That, of course, lands us squarely into the issue of activity on the analyst's part, something that is forbidden by the whole system of conceptualization that may be summarized under the concept of neutrality. The way that problem often appears, as it does in the monograph edited by Dowling, is under the concept of "corrective emotional experience," which I deal with elsewhere in this volume.

It must be noted that the concept of compromise formation is usually – and surely in the monograph I mentioned – treated as solely an intrapsychic one. Competing forces within the mind reach a compromise. Such a concept, of course, seriously deemphasizes the role of experience, that is, of the external world, except insofar as it is intrapsychically represented.

There is no necessary connection between the *Freudian* concept of drive and conflict, although such a connection is often implied. I will return to the question of the inevitability of conflict in my discussion of the theory of motivation.

"Deficit" is only a way of referring to a less than optimal environment. To deny deficit in favor of conflict is only a way of insisting that conflict is inevitable even in the most favorable of environments. Those who emphasize conflict of course deal with deficit too and those who emphasize deficit deal with conflict too. As I said, a self psychologist who deals with a patient's inability to accept mirroring, or whatever, is in the realm of conflict too. The terms are really buzzwords to indicate whether one's allegiance is primarily to the effects of unfavorable experience or primarily with the inevitability of conflict, whatever the experience. Is this so different from insisting primarily on the importance of trauma or primarily on the importance of constitution? Surely the relative proportion of each must be decided in the individual case, but they must both be always important.

3

One-Person and Two-Person
Psychology

One of the major, more specific ways in which the relationship between the internal and the external has been argued in psychoanalysis is whether it is a one-person or a two-person psychology. The intrapsychic structure—with its varying proportion of innate and internalized experiential—can be conceptualized as a relatively closed system, addressable through a one-person psychology. If, on the other hand, primary attention is given to the interaction between external and internal, the conceptualization is of an open, two-person psychology or, better, since the experiential is more than the interpersonal, a two-factor conceptualization. And, to repeat, it must never be forgotten that psychoanalytically, the external factor must be dealt with as it is *experienced*, not in behavioral terms.

Self psychology, by making the self superordinate, in that sense emphasizes a one-person psychology. The self-psychological emphasis on talents and ideals (although both, of course, are experientially influenced) is also a one-person emphasis. The emphasis on experience in self psychology makes it a two-person psychology as well (Gill, 1994b).

As criticism of mainstream psychoanalysis has grown with more and more emphasis on object relations, there has been what many would regard as an overshooting of the mark, with a replacement of a one-person view of the analytic situation by a two-person view. As balance is being restored, the question becomes, are both one- and two-person psychologies necessary, and, if so, how are they related?

First a distinction must be made between an individual psyche and the analytic situation. *Manifestly* the first is one person while the second involves two people. Does the study of one person require a two-person psychology as well as a one? Does the study of the analytic situation require a one-person psychology as well as a two?

Freud's theory has always had both one-person and two-person aspects. At first, in its one-person aspect, psychopathology was due to dammed up affect, which had to be discharged. This was Freud's initial catharsis theory. In its two-person aspect, the theory was interpersonal. Freud considered that trauma in interpersonal relationships was responsible for psychopathology. This is the view of the early work *Studies on Hysteria* (Breuer and Freud, 1893–1895). Trauma soon became narrowed to sexual trauma in the period of the childhood seduction theory of psychopathology. And, finally, with the discovery that many of the tales of seduction were fantasies, came the theory of instinctual drive. It is the emphasis on drive, even though issues concerning relationships with people always loomed large in Freudian writing, that leads to the characterization of psychoanalysis as a one-person psychology. Mainstream Freudians often regard this characterization of psychoanalysis as grossly skewed precisely because there is so much consideration of interpersonal relationships in psychoanalysis. I will later discuss in detail an important reason that mainstream psychoanalysis is nevertheless reasonably regarded as a one-person psychology, but a few remarks about it here.

In psychoanalytic theory an external event is often considered a matter of social psychology, the event coming under the purview of psychoanalysis only in terms of its intrapsychic meaning. It is this latter assumption that has been misunderstood as making psychoanalysis a one-person psychology. But external events remain important. It is true that it is impossible to say how important in the psyche an event may be until one learns how the subject experiences it. It is even true that certain events that one might expect to be important to everyone are not important to a particular person. But that does not diminish the importance of external events as a class. It is the latter that is the central emphasis of the interpersonal school—the importance of events as a class and the class of interpersonal events in particular.

In the light of the centrality of the concept of transference in psychoanalysis, one might think that the analytic situation which Freud invented would have been understood as between two people, or as it has come to be known, a two-person situation. I say the "invention" of the psychoanalytic situation by Freud because never before had anyone thought of asking two people to relate to one another such that one of them tried to speak what passed through his mind as freely as possible while the other one devoted himself essentially to understanding the psychology of the first person and conveying that understanding to him.

Clearly it was only in a therapeutic context that such an arrangement could have been invented, for why other than in the hope of relief from suffering would one person be willing to relate to another person in that way? Of course, the analytic situation has its precursors. People have doubtless unburdened themselves to friends and received advice ever since the beginning of the human race. And the analytic situation has been more specifically compared to the Catholic confessional.

But the differences between such precursors and the analytic situation are major ones. One does not bind oneself to speak as freely as possible to a friend, and the analyst is alleged to offer only understanding, not advice. The priest, of course, offers forgiveness and requires contrition. A connection between understanding and forgiveness may be seen in the aphorism that to understand is to forgive.

TRANSFERENCE

The more specific discussion of the one-person versus two-person controversy in psychoanalysis has dealt mainly with the transference. When I wrote my monograph on transference (Gill, 1982) I did not realize that I was discussing a more specific version of the one-person–two-person controversy, nor indeed that the controversy is a more specific aspect of the innate–experiential (internal–external) controversy.

Every educated person is familiar with the idea of transference: the patient relates to the therapist as he related to those influential in his rearing. Surely one would then understand the analytic situation as a relationship between two people. But, in fact, that understanding has been generally accepted only comparatively recently, so recently that it is still disputed whether the analytic situation – and transference – should be understood, in terms used by Michael Balint (1953), as a one-person or a two-person psychology.

The transference was long understood not as a relationship between analyst and analysand, but rather as a *distortion* by the analysand of the situation between analyst and analysand. I say "distortion of the situation" rather than "distortion of the relationship" because to speak of a relationship presumes two people involved with one another, whereas the long–held view of transference was not one of a relationship between two people, but rather of the distorted view of the analyst by the analysand.

How was that possible? I think for two reasons: an intellectual one, that the medical model of a doctor acting upon a patient but not involved in an interaction was taken over into the psychoanalytic, and even the psychotherapeutic, situation, especially as practiced by medical doctors; and an emotional one, that the intense affective interplay between analyst and analysand, inevitable in a situation of psychological therapy, had to be denied by both participants.

I believe it can be demonstrated that the classical definition of transference is false even on purely logical grounds. For it is the analyst who declares what the transference is, and surely a basic tenet of psychoanalysis is that we can never be unequivocally certain of our own motivations. His declaration therefore must be a construction; that is, he has participated in its formation. It might be argued against this that while the analyst may conclude what the patient's transference is, that might still be the conclusion of an uninvolved bystander. But the issue is not whether the analyst is correct but whether he recognizes that he has contributed to what he is now passing judgment on. Again I offer the same two counterarguments: an intellectual one, that the analyst participates in an analytic situation already makes him a contributor; and an emotional one, that experience has shown that the analyst is either involved or defending against being involved. And the latter is a kind of involvement too.

The argument as to whether the analytic situation should be understood as a one-person or a two-person psychology is more familiarly discussed in terms of whether or not the analyst is a mirror (or, as it is sometimes put, a blank screen). In the usual classical formula first enunciated by Freud, the analyst is a blank screen or a mirror, reflecting back only what comes from the patient, although everyone knows that Freud himself was anything but a blank screen. Of course, the absurdity of such a view, its utter confounding by actual experience, could not long be overlooked. So various critiques of the blank screen began to appear. They have been described in a classic paper by Hoffman (1983), who divided them into a standard view and conservative and radical critiques. The title of his paper signals what it is about. He called it "The Patient as Interpreter of the Analyst's Experience." According to "standard qualifications of the blank screen concept," the patient is seen as responding realistically to the analyst's expertise and benevolence within, following Freud (1912), the friendly, even affectionate transference, the so-called unobjectionable positive transference. Also the patient is seen as responding realistically to blatant intrusions of countertransference. Conservative critics build on these standard qualifications, arguing that they deserve more emphasis and elaboration. Some emphasize that countertransference is very common, although they regard it as an unfortunate violation of appropriate neutrality (of which more soon) that can be overcome by diligent analysis of the analyst.

The conservative critiques also promote a humane, helpful stance by the analyst—an acceptable, even desirable, deviation from the blank-screen stance. Some no longer see it as part of transference, as Freud did, but instead they propose a variety of alliance concepts or a variety of conceptions of the analyst's benign, therapeutic influence. Recently, Nella Guidi (1993) of Italy proposed an unobjectionable negative transference in parallel with the unobjectionable positive transference. Similarly, I suggest, one can think of unobjectionable positive and negative countertransference.

The radical critics of the blank screen are, in effect, constructivist. They argue that necessarily an analyst's experience is ambiguous, that it is influenced by the patient's "interpretations" of it (hitherto his "fantasies"), which can be usefully considered as palusible constructions. The latter may be quite selective and neurotically driven, however.

It is tempting to see the analyst's contribution to the transference as "great" or "small," but that is a very dangerous temptation. It easily leads to the notion that if the contribution is small, perhaps it is of no importance and maybe can be wiped out altogether. But it cannot be small. The setup of the psychotherapeutic situation itself is sponsored by, and thus signifies a massive contribution by, the therapist. It is not only his interpretations that should be viewed as constructions; his understanding of the very nature of the situation is a construction. While it is true that the difference between how the two participants experience the relationship may seem great or small from the point of view of an external observer, the really important point is the meaning of the difference to the two participants and what they see their respective contributions to be. In fact, to use quantitative consider-ations at all may be an illogical mix of positivist and relativist perspectives.

A vivid illustration by Levenson (1991) comes to mind. The patient accuses the therapist of having poisoned his soup. The therapist is sure he has made no contribution to this delusional idea. Of course, he has not fed the patient any soup (shades of Freud feeding herring to the Rat Man!) much less poisoned soup. But what if this is a metaphor for the patient's experience of having been fed poisoned interpretations?

Constructivism not only implies that the analyst makes a contri-bution to the patient's experience, but also that the patient's experi-ence is ambiguous, that the sources of the analyst's views and actions are not fully known, and that analyst and patient act to cocreate interactional realities, both through enactments in transference and countertransference and through searching for new ways of being in relationships. I derive these formulations from Hoffman's writings.

Lipton (1977) has argued that analyst and analysand have two different kinds of relationship. He makes his case in the context of his view that modern technique is a change for the worse from Freud's techniques, and he illustrates this claim by comparing retrogressive modern technique with Freud's technique in his treatment of the Rat Man. As Lipton puts it, "the essence of the difference between modern technique and Freud's is that the definition of technique has been expanded to incorporate aspects of the analyst's relation with the patient which Freud excluded from technique" (p. 162). Lipton does emphasize that these aspects of the analyst's relation to the patient, which Freud allegedly excluded from technique (although Freud wrote only of the "unobjectionable positive transference") *"by no means imply that their repercussions are excluded from the analysis. On the contrary . . . "* (p. 259). He ascribes the departure from Freud's "rela-tional" technique largely to a reaction against Franz Alexander's (1956) proposals to manipulate the transference rather than to analyze it.

While that may well have been a factor in the change, I am inclined to emphasize the growing recognition of how any behavior on the analyst's part can be responded to in ways that belie his or her conscious intentions. To avoid thus "contaminating" the transference, analysts came to progressively restrict their behavior. Apfelbaum (1966) made the same point in discussing analysts' recognition that any direct attempt to expose a patient's unconscious wishes would be unwise. But instead of responding to this recognition by an expansion of ego (defense) analysis, many analysts responded by keeping interpretation itself to a minimum. The result was a withdrawal from overt interaction with the patient and thus a move away from Freud's (1926) conception of the analytic process as a conversation. The latter implies a two-person situation as against an altered and regressive monologue, which implies a one-person situation. I have argued elsewhere (Gill, 1982) that the fact that the analytic situation is an interpersonal one makes withdrawal impossible in principle. I will later argue that the analyst should not only be more ready to make defense interpretations, that is, interpretations from the "side of the ego," but should also permit himself a greater degree of spontaneity with the recognition that there will inevitably be transference–countertransference consequences that need analysis (Hoffman, 1992a). Paul Gray (1982) has also emphasized the common failure to analyze defense adequately. He calls it a lag in technique. Apfelbaum and I (1989) have also addressed this topic, emphasizing especially that any particular content can be impulse or defense (see also Gill, 1963).

I must emphasize that I have been discussing the analytic *situation*, not the psychology of an individual human being. I agree, that is, with Leo Stone (1961), who observed that "we must still recognize that theoretic considerations based largely on the psychoanalytic psychology of the individual (i.e., the patient) should be supplemented by special considerations derived from the dynamic situation itself" (p. 10).

There are those who argue that human individuality comes into being only by way of interpersonal interaction, and others who argue that this view obscures, at least in terms of what is innate, that which belongs solely to a one-person psychology. I reviewed some of these arguments when I discussed the relationship between the internal and the external, one variant of this dichotomy being the innate and the experiential.

If we ask whether human psychology involves more than a relationship with other people, the answer seems obvious. Important though relationships with other people are, there is much more to life than that. That the analytic situation involves two people may be a factor in overvaluing the role of relations with people as the alleged core of psychic life. That relationships with people are intrapsychically represented may also be a factor in undervaluing other aspects of the human psyche.

Intertwining issues of relationships with persons with all the other aspects of psychological functioning may be yet another factor in the failure to recognize these other aspects. And yet another possibility: because psychopathology is so often a matter of relationships, other aspects of human functioning may be overlooked.

As Emmanuel Ghent (1989) points out: "Kohut . . . added the dimension of talents, ideals, and ambitions, and in so doing tended to shift the emphasis in the direction of a one-person psychology, in contrast with the object relations and interpersonal theorists whose emphasis rests solidly on goals of human interaction. In fact, a weakness of these latter theories is that they hardly dealt with issues that were not directly interhuman" (p. 193). Of course Kohut's emphasis on the self likewise shifts the emphasis toward a one-person psychology. It is noteworthy that many self psychologists deny how heavily their theory is *also* interpersonal, for fear, I think, that they will not be considered proper intrapsychic psychoanalysts (Gill, 1994b).

For the time being, I assert only that psychoanalysis needs both one-person and two-person psychologies (Ghent, 1989). It is important to note that this discussion of one-person and two-person psychologies has been with regard to the *theories* of the analytic situation. In actual practice, analysts have always, to varying degrees, pragmatically worked in both one-person and two-person contexts.

ALLIANCE CONCEPTS

A somewhat grudging concession by classical analysts to the view of the analytic situation as a two-person relationship is the concept an alliance between analyst and analysand. While that concept doubtless goes back to antiquity, its modern usage, at least insofar as psychoanalysis and psychoanalytic psychotherapy are concerned, goes back to Freud. He spoke of analysis as a collaboration between analyst and analysand, without which analysis was not possible. One of the ways Freud expressed this was in his distinction between the transference neuroses and the nonanalyzable psychoses. Transference neurosis in this sense was a nosological designation rather than the more commonly content-related notion of transference neurosis as the recapitulation of the infantile neurosis.

As a nosological designation, transference neuroses, for Freud, were those disorders which were treatable by psychoanalysis because the patient was capable of forming an object relationship, that is, a transference to the therapist. Analogously, I believe that an analyst has to form a countertransference (a relationship) to the patient to create an analytic situation. Freud spoke of the psychoses as not analyzable because transference failed to develop. That formulation has been altered in present-day thinking to one in which the psychoses are not analyzable because the transference is too overwhelming; that is to say, there is no reality-oriented relationship with the analyst as a context within which the patient's view of the analyst can be examined and altered. The more overwhelming the transference, the less the patient can distinguish one person or one therapist from another.

Alliance concepts became explicit prominently in the work of Zetzel (1956), Greenson (1965), and Sandler, Dare, and Holder (1973). The names given to the alliance by these writers differed somewhat, being called, respectively, therapeutic alliance, working alliance, and treatment alliance.

Most psychoanalysts and psychotherapists seem to have accepted these alliance concepts as useful and important, although, in so doing, they only make explicit what had been implicit in analytic theory and practice from the beginning. I believe that the rise to explicit prominence of the alliance concept was an attempt to correct what had come to be considered the overly rigid, withdrawn, silent stance of the analyst. This rigid stance was, to some degree at least, an effort to differentiate sharply psychoanalysis and psychotherapy, as a more interactive, demonstrative stance was considered supportive, reassuring, and opposed to the goal of analysis as designed solely to bring about insight. An important landmark in the swing of the pendulum to counteract this overly rigid stance was Leo Stone's (1961) monograph The Psychoanalytic Situation. Stone pointed out that this stance, often caricatured in the lay press, especially in cartoons, not to mention in professional writings, led to an unnecessary, iatrogenic regression, although he agreed with the generally accepted idea that a significant regression is a necessary part of the psychoanalytic process. At the same time, Stone emphasized what he called the analysand's irredentist urge to return to the mother. He regarded some gratification of this urge as necessary and inevitable, but, since his monograph preceded the work of those who explicitly emphasized an alliance, he did not discuss the matter under that name.

The outstanding formulation of the rigid stance was by Kurt Eissler (1953). He argued that any deviation from pure interpretation was a "parameter" and that any such parameter had to be resolved to zero by interpretation if the therapy was to be designated true psychoanalysis. That analytic climate has long grown away from such a stance and continues to do so even further, was clearly evidenced at a panel on Eissler's concept at the December 1992 meeting of the American Psychoanalytic Association. The self-psychological emphasis on a "friendlier" ambience in the analytic situation (Wolf, 1988) is further evidence of that trend.

A contemporary version of the alliance concept is the notion of the so-called holding environment. The concept was originated by Winnicott (1971) and is currently championed by Modell (1990). It is given special prominence in the treatment of sicker patients. The concept of holding is that the therapist avoids any probing analytic work, possibly for a long period of time, until the patient acquires enough trust in the therapist for such work to begin. Once again, those who argue for holding often offer little explicit discussion of the fact that such holding is an unverbalized interaction, contrary to the analytic tenets of avoiding interaction and analysis of the interaction that does take place. Of course, one might counter that the holding environment is necessary until such time as probing analytic work can be done, but there also does not seem to be adequate recognition that at some point, the significance of the prior holding requires examination. This is a point I will pursue in more detail in discussing whether the transference must be analyzed immediately and relentlessly from the very beginning or, for that matter, at any point when the analyst believes he discerns it.

Kohut (1984), too, recommended sometimes withholding analysis of the patient's need for mirroring or idealization, perhaps for quite a long time. But he did recommend its eventual analysis. I wonder if he meant to include making explicit the patient's experience of the prior withholding as well as the change in tactics.

It is often not recognized that Freud recommended fostering, or at least requiring, an alliance as crucial to psychoanalytic work, because, although he later used the term alliance casually, he gave it a different name at first. He called it the unobjectionable positive transference

(Freud, 1912b) (and later the patient–analyst collaboration [Freud, 1940]). Freud felt that the unobjectionable positive transference was essential to maintaining the analytic process. By the unobjectionable positive transference, he meant a true transference, that is, an importation into the analytic situation of a pattern of relationship based in the past. It is sometimes not recognized that this is a "true" transference because, contrary to the incorrect but widely held view of transference, it does not seem to be a distortion of the current patient–analyst relationship but rather a "rational" adaptation to it. The fact that it may be a highly *selective* response to the analytic situation is often readily apparent, for a plausible response to the analytic situation, surely at the beginning, would be a cautious testing of this new relationship to see what it is like. Wholehearted trust based on the fact that one is in the hands of a licensed practitioner, even one of excellent reputation, is hardly the only possible adaptive response. Yet it is this unobjectionable positive transference that, for Freud, is the main reason the analysand will even listen to the analyst at all, particularly when the analyst confronts him with ideas he would rather not hear about.

But surely *some* degree of trust is necessary, even just to start with. Whether or not it will grow depends on whether or not it is warranted by what happens. Even then, it will be tested in the storms of negative transference as well as in the less obvious defensive idealization. The alliance, then, is an *outgrowth* of the work if it goes well. An unequivocal and complete trust at the very beginning of an analysis should be a warning of the distrust that it may well conceal.

Martin Stein (1981) has written a very good paper on how the apparently unobjectionable positive transference can serve as a major resistance. The phenomenon may be especially evident in a training analysis, in which the candidate is often dependent on the analyst for advancement in his career and is therefore loath to antagonize him.

Stone's (1961) monograph was an important step toward the revision of the concept of the analyst as an uninvolved bystander. It was particularly important in helping me overcome my classical training. I have never forgotten this remark in the midst of his careful, rather pedantic presentation: "The enthusiastic and engaging [!] assertion of an older colleague many years ago that his patient would have developed the same vivid transference love toward him 'if he had been a brass monkey' is alas (or, perhaps, fortunately!) just not true." (p. 41)

The alliance concept, as noted earlier, is fairly widely accepted as an important way of conceptualizing an aspect of the patient–therapist relationship, not only in psychotherapy, but in psychoanalysis as well. It was sometimes discussed, especially by Greenson (1965), in terms of the analyst's being more overtly humane, rather than rigidly detached. He also emphasized that there is a reality relationship between patient and therapist in addition to the "irrational" transference.

There were some dissenting voices, however, notably Kanzer (1975), Brenner (1979), Curtis (1979), and Stein (1981). They considered the alliance, at least as it was being conceptualized by Greenson and Zetzel, to dangerously veer toward psychotherapy and away from analysis, in that it seemed to be employed as a reassuring device. While they did not deny that reassurance and support play a role in the analytic process, they argued that these attitudes are inherent ingredients of the analytic process and that the effort to isolate them as something to be *fostered* risks being a manipulation without subsequent analysis of how such attitudes are implicated in both transference and countertransference.

Some justification for this dissenting view lies in the work of Zetzel (1970), who regarded active steps for the development of such an alliance as *preliminary* to the analytic work proper. Furthermore, preliminary though it might be, she did not make explicit any need for the subsequent analysis of these steps taken for support and reassurance.

Brenner (1979), in particular, reviewed the clinical instances given by Greenson and Zetzel to show how, in his view, these nonanalytic activities were not only unnecessary but potentially harmful. For example, Brenner suggested that if an analyst were to express sympathy on hearing a patient's announcement of the death of a relative, the analyst might thereby be inhibiting the patient from expressing negative feelings about the relative, conceivably even relief and pleasure at the death. Brenner clearly implied that the appropriate stance is silence, waiting to hear the patient's associations.

SILENCE AS AN INTERACTION

What seems to me to be omitted in Brenner's account is the possible implications of being silent. The patient might regard silence as a grave lack of sympathy. Brenner might very well counter that if that is the

case such a reaction would be material to be analyzed. The implication, however, is that such a reaction would be an irrational transference. Perhaps more important, the implication is that if the analyst
says nothing, he is doing nothing.

My argument is that even if the analyst says *nothing*, he is doing
something; that is to say, he is remaining silent in the face of what may
well be a major event in the patient's life. Again Brenner might
counter that the patient has presumably learned that the purpose of
the analysis is not to provide sympathy but to analyze the patient's
reactions. Again, I do not disagree. But I do suggest that the patient's
reactions may very well be concealed in his associations, an implicit
reaction of pleasure, for example, that the analyst has not inhibited
him from expressing negative feelings he has about the death, or
perhaps, implicit anger with the analyst for his silence in the face of
this major event. Brenner might again counter that he would be alert
to such implications in the patient's associations and make the necessary interpretation. I believe he probably would often do that. But my
view is that unless an analyst is thoroughly convinced of the interpersonal nature of the analytic situation, he may not be alert to the fact
that there must be *some* personal response on the patient's part (as well
as on the analyst's part). This response by the patient may very well be
hidden because the patient has probably been schooled to accept the
analyst's silence as the proper way of proceeding and to consider that
were he to complain about the analyst's failure to express sympathy,
his complaint would be attributed to an irrational insistence on
violating the rules of analysis.

How, then, would I recommend that such a situation be handled? I
offer no rule as to whether or not there should be an expression of
sympathy or, indeed, as to whether or not anything should be said.
What I emphasize is that there will be interpersonal significance for
both analyst and analysand in *whatever* the analyst does or does not
do, and that the analyst must be alert to these interpersonal meanings.
They will often be expressed only indirectly in his or her interventions
and the patient's associations.

A possible overt response by the therapist might be to say, "How do
you feel about it?" This would seem to convey to the patient that there
is no particular way he must necessarily respond to the death. He need
not conventionally grieve nor is he prevented from expressing pleasure. Of course, the question "How do you feel about it?" may also be

how the therapist defends himself against his interpersonal reaction, against being considered cold and unfeeling, for example. This question will also elicit some kind of a response, again very possibly implicit rather than explicit. For example, the patient, if he allows himself to be conscious of it, may feel, "There's that damned blank inquiry again, as if the analyst has no feelings about it." My point remains then. There is no such thing as an intervention, including silence, that is not at the same time an action that arises from an interpersonal response and to which there will be an interpersonal response in return (Gill, in Oremland, 1991).

Brenner's conceptualization of the situation implies a gratification–frustration index whereby the patient may respond to the analyst's stance with either gratification or frustration. His position suggests that the safe thing to do is to frustrate. If he does indeed take such a position, I would argue that he thereby violates the central psychoanalytic tenet that one should not manipulate the transference. But if I insist that every intervention, including silence, is an action, how can I say that the transference should not be manipulated? The answer is that I understand a manipulation to be only a *witting* intervention that the analyst does not intend to analyze. Neither an *unwitting* suggestion nor a witting suggestion that one intends to analyze, if possible, constitutes "manipulation." But I want the analyst to consider silence a witting intervention.

Deliberate frustration without the intention to analyze it is a manipulation. And how can one be sure what the effect of an interpersonal manipulation will be? It is not possible to say beforehand what the patient will experience as frustrating or gratifying. An often-used example of that fact is that, whereas most of us presumably would feel that if a man stopped beating his wife she would be relieved, it is also possible that her milieu or personality might be such that she would be terribly upset because she would consider his no longer beating her an indication that he no longer loves her, or at any rate, has lost interested in her.

The countertransference problems involved in the clinical illustration offered by Brenner also need to be considered. The failure to make a response to the announcement of a death could be a rationalization of a sadistic motive. It could also be an expression of empathy on the analyst's part in that he might recognize that for this particular patient an expression of sympathy would indeed inhibit the expression of pleasure. But the analyst may find it humanly difficult to refrain from some sympathetic remark in the face of the announcement of a death. Were he to follow prescribed analytic technique and remain silent, that might in itself make him so uncomfortable that he would have difficulty in dealing with the patient's complaint about his silence, if there should be a complaint. He would then be even more inclined to regard the complaint as an irrational transference. This, in turn, could lead him to overlook the contribution he has made to the patient's response, namely, his silence, especially if the patient's interpersonal response to the silence were only implicit in his or her associations.

My thesis is that the therapist should embrace the principle that whatever he does or does not do is an action that will have its interpersonal meaning, that he has a major responsibility to search for this meaning, and, in interpreting that meaning, to recognize that his response (and here silence is a response) is a stimulus to bring about a response on the analysand's part. And the analysand's response will not simply be an irrational reaction without any basis in the ongoing interaction.

Of course, it is not possible to say whether the therapist's silence is a rationalization of a sadistic motive, or his expression of sympathy is an expression of a compulsion to be "motherly," or whatever. Once again, one cannot assess a behavior without knowing how it is intrapsychically experienced. And it is the patient who is in analysis, not the therapist. One can only hope that the therapist's personal analysis has acquainted him with himself and that his conduct of an analysis is pursued with a continuing self-analysis. I believe that even if an analyst is subjectively comfortable with his silence because he feels he is simply following correct technique, his silence still has interpersonal meanings to himself, however preconscious or unconscious they may be.

One of the ways in which the ideal of the noncontributing therapist has been described is his "neutrality." My review of this concept in the next chapter will open a more general consideration of the notion of analytic interaction and its relationship to interpretation.

4

Neutrality

Neutrality has been much discussed in the psychoanalytic literature. I have already said that in its extreme form, the analyst is supposed to be like a screen or like a mirror, reflecting back to the patient only what has come from the patient.

A nonanalytic therapy that attempts to put this precept of neutrality into practice is nondirective, or client-centered, psychotherapy (Rogers, 1951), once much in vogue among psychologists. For legal reasons probably, what are usually called patients were called clients by these practitioners. Client-centered therapists often spoke very critically of what they considered to be the heavy-handed imposition by analysts of their own concepts and values onto victimized patients. Psychoanalysts, in turn, ridiculed client-centered therapists for what they regarded as passivity. I remember one caricature that went like this: A suicidal patient finally jumps out of the window in the therapist's office. The therapist has been saying, "You feel suicidal. Now you feel like walking over to the window. Now you feel like jumping out of the window. There you go!"

While nondirective therapy had the merit of attempting to really understand the patient's psychic reality (Schwaber, 1992), its insistence that the therapist not impose himself at all on the patient was a denial that the therapeutic situation is a dyad and that such nonimposition is impossible. The therapist's selection of what to reflect back out of the patient's total communication is already a pivotal contribution to the relationship. A review of nondirective therapy protocols reveals this fatal flaw most clearly in the therapist's failure to pick up on implicit, or even blatantly explicit, references to the transference.

Most current definitions of neutrality are based on the blank-screen model, even as modified by a conservative critique of that model. The definition most often cited is Anna Freud's (1956). She said that the analyst remains equidistant from id, ego, and superego, that is, does not takes sides with any one of the three divisions of the personality. All this means, in effect, is that the analyst reflects back only what comes from the patient. Fenichel (1941, p. 70) took exception to this formula, saying that the analyst always works with the ego and reaches the id and superego by way of the ego. Hence, said Fenichel, he is closer to the ego than to id or superego. Recently Levy and Inderbitzin (1992) suggested that neutrality should be not only to id, ego, and superego but to external reality as well. But in essence they maintain the blank-screen view (Gill, 1994c).

What is really a caricature of neutrality, though not always recognized as such, is what has been called behavioral neutrality (Lipton, 1977; Apfelbaum and Gill, 1989). Indeed, it is that feature of analysis most often caricatured in cartoons in the lay press. The analyst is silent. The reason for the silence has been called "the second fundamental rule": "*Analytic treatment should be carried through, as far as possible, under privation—in a state of abstinence*. . . . It is expedient to deny him [the patient] precisely those satisfactions which he desires most intensely and expresses most importunately" (Freud, 1919, pp. 162, 164).

Many analysts seem to regard the analyst's silence as his doing nothing and hence maintaining neutrality. Only a fixation on the idea that the analyst is uninvolved could lead anyone to be so blind. Menninger's (1958) textbook dealt with the analyst's silence in a way that makes clear that it is an action designed to frustrate the patient. It is not neutral at all.

Apfelbaum and I (1989) proposed the concept of "interpretive neutrality," stemming from our suggestion that an important technical conclusion from structural theory is that a particular mental content may be an impulse toward a content closer to ego syntonicity and a defense against a content further from ego syntonicity, and that the analyst should interpret what is closest to the ego. But that formulation is really the same as Fenichel's concept of always working from the side of the ego.

How, then, is neutrality to be defined? I suggest the answer follows from taking seriously the dyadic nature of the therapeutic situation. The analyst is *always* influencing the patient, and the patient is *always* influencing the analyst. This mutual influence cannot be avoided; it can only be interpreted. It is the analyst's awareness of this unremitting influence of patient and analyst on each other and his attempt to make that influence as explicit as possible that constitute his "neutrality."

Heinrich Racker (1968) expressed the same idea by arguing that the analyst always has a countertransference neurosis in the analytic situation. Its nature varies according to the analyst's interaction with the particular analysand. I submit that the neutral analyst is the analyst who continuously self-analyzes his countertransference neurosis (with the help of the patient's associations) in parallel with his analysis of the patient's transference, again understanding the latter (and the former!) to be contributed to by both participants and who attempts to deal with the effect of his countertransference on the analytic situation as fully as possible. By this, I do not mean necessarily by this an explicit disclosure of his countertransference, a subject I will turn to later.

Interesting definitions of neutrality from an interpersonal point of view have been offered by Greenberg (1986) and Aron (1991)). The analyst maintains a balance between being available to the patient as an "old" and as a "new" object (Hoffman, 1991). In Aron's words, "In Piagetian terms the analyst's neutrality facilitates the equilibrium between assimilation and accommodation which enables optimal growth and adaptation" (p. 105). Of course, to speak of the analyst's "availability" may imply witting maneuvers that are not analyzed.

I have expressed my objections to a discussion of neutrality by Levy and Inderbitzen (1992) in a letter to the *Journal of the American Psychoanalytic Association* (Gill, 1994c).

I will later, in discussing spontaneity on the analyst's part, raise the question of how his role is to be distinguished from an ordinary social one, if it is granted that the analyst is always affectively involved in the analytic situation. Is there no room for the conception of a neutral analyst? An answer can be found in the application of of a general concept of dialectic interweaving of what at first appear to be polar opposites (Hoffman, 1991, 1994). In the analytic situation, there is always the context that any interaction may subsequently be the subject of examination, that is, analysis. The noninvolvement of the analyst, then, finds expression in the potential for analysis of any interaction, even if this potential is in the background at any particular time.

INTERACTION AND INTERPRETATION

Interpretation is one of the chief examples of an intervention whose interactive nature can be overlooked. When an analyst makes an interpretation, his conscious sense is that he is merely pointing something out with no intention of making a suggestion to the patient. But reflection should make clear that it is impossible to make an interpretation that is not at the same time a suggestion or, otherwise put, an action. Since the same is true for the analysand's influence on the analyst, the analytic situation can be described as an interaction, or as Stolorow and his colleagues (1987) put it in the light of constructivism, an intersubjective interaction.

The patient experiences the interpretation, whether consciously or not, both as an imparting of insight and as an action. Perhaps the most obvious implication of many interpretations is a suggestion to alter a particular behavior or feeling. The statement "You are afraid of expressing your anger" is likely to be experienced as "Stop being so afraid and express your anger." "You find my silence distressing just as you experienced your father as distant and unapproachable" is likely to be experienced as meaning "My silence is just part of the analytic method. If you experience it as distressing, that is because you irrationally equate it with your father's apparent distance and unapproachability. Stop misinterpreting me." I once organized a research protocol around how interpretations are interpersonally experienced.

Not only interpretations, but all verbal and nonverbal behaviors of the analyst, are experienced as actions by the patient (Namnum, 1976). "Umhm" can be a powerful reassurance. The relative minimization of behavioral action by the analyst makes his overt actions an even more significant contribution to the therapeutic situation. Does the analyst snatch the napkin off the pillow before the patient has left the room? Does he smile when he says hello? *Does* he say hello? Does he hand the bill to the patient personally, or does he mail it? Is he prompt with the bill? And a million other pieces of behavior, any one of which can acquire great significance in the patient's experience. Analysts recognize, of course, that gross behaviors on their part, like forgetting a patient's appointment or just being a few minutes late for it, can have great importance to a patient, but the same principle applies to all the analyst's behavior, not just these gross instances.

Of course, an overriding source of the analyst's contribution to the situation lies in his person and his office. In Chicago the story is often told of a WASP banker who looked startled when the analyst's door opened for the first time and he saw a small, not too well dressed little man who appeared obviously Jewish. "Come in, come in, anyhow," said the analyst.

Phyllis Greenacre (1954) some years ago advised that the analyst's office should be spare and bare. She also believed that an analyst should not participate in any public activity, such as taking a position on an issue, if it might be publicized. When I was a resident, there was a heated discussion among the staff as to whether it was permissible for a staff member or a resident, or even a wife of one of them, to take a role in the local amateur theater. One analytic institute refused a woman permission to take an extension course because it was taught by an analysand of her husband. In my first course in analytic technique, the instructor, whom I shall mercifully not name, said that in the ideal analytic situation the analyst would be behind a screen and his or her voice would be disguised so that the patient would not know the sex of the analyst. Furthermore, as it soon became clear, the disguise would hardly be necessary for the first several hundred hours because the analyst should preferably say nothing during that time anyhow. I suspect the reader will think I am making all this up. I am not. The only place where I have shaded the truth is that the instructor said the analyst should say *almost* nothing for the first several hundred hours. And although he described the ideal analytic situation as one using an actual screen, he did not tell us to use one. In fairness, I should say that he did not offer these strictures as embodiments of neutrality, but as tactics designed to frustrate the patient to regress so that the required analytic material would appear. Actually, in his own work, he often read his mail and played chess by mail during analytic sessions!

Another word on the analyst's silence: I have already several times mentioned how extraordinary it is that many analysts seem to believe that the silent analyst is doing nothing. Of course, the silence can be construed by the patient in a multitude of ways, from stubborn withholding, to thoughtful attentiveness, to empathic abstention from rude intrusiveness.

It is sometimes suggested that if all intervention is also interaction, the analytic situation can become an infinite regress. I mean this in the sense that if one interprets the interactive significance of an interaction, that interpretation has an interactive significance too. Can one then never escape interaction? No, but the meaning of the interaction can change. For example, an interpretation of homosexuality may be experienced by a patient as a homosexual assault. If the interpretation is then made that the interpretation has been experienced as a homosexual assault, this may again be experienced as a homosexual assault. What does one do then?

I suggest that the second interpretation is likely to have a different interactive significance from the first. The second is an insensitive repetition of the interpretation rather than an examination of how the first was experienced as an assault. Presumably, in time it will be possible to make an interpretation of homosexuality that will be experienced not as a homosexual assault but as an attempt to help the patient to an insight.

Although interaction never ends, its interpretation does reach a point of diminishing returns in the clinical sense that, once certain major interactive themes and patterns implicated in the patient's psychopathology have been well analyzed and worked through, the patient has gotten as much out of analysis as he can reasonably expect to get and must go on with his life. One of the goals of analytic treatment is understanding that everything we say and don't say, do and don't do, in interpersonal relations has interactive implications; such understanding could be called a procedural goal in contrast to the understanding of a specific interaction.

I add several points about the injunction to interpret the interaction. The injunction can itself lead to a perversion of the analytic process in that the insistence on interpreting every jot and tittle of the interaction can itself become a major interaction with an unfortunate effect on the analysis. It must be assumed that much in the interaction will simply pass by, but I believe the major themes of the interaction will be often repeated and will become the focus of analytic work if the analyst is convinced of the principle I am espousing. This is especially true of what is regularly, perhaps even always, a major and often unrecognized interaction, namely, how analyst and analysand conceive of the nature of the analytic process. This interaction and probably most, if not all, interactions are most commonly realized and interpreted only retrospectively by the analyst who has for some time been immersed in them (Renik, 1993).

Because of the emphasis I have placed on the analysis of the interaction in the here-and-now, it is often mistakenly concluded that I see no value in reconstructions of the past. I believe that there is often value in such reconstructions, though, of course, I also believe that such reconstructions are also constructions in the sense in which I earlier spoke of constructivism. While a reconstruction can occasionally be a path to the illumination of the here-and-now, I believe it is usually the here-and-now that is the path to the past. Of course, a reconstruction that binds the here-and-now and the past together is likely to be the most effective interpretation of all.

Ronald Ganellen (personal communication) argues that knowledge of the patient's developmental history can be valuable in determining which of various themes in the here-and-now is the best one to pursue. In considering the role of extratransference interpretation, it is important to distinguish between current extratransference and genetic extratransference. The former is more likely to conceal transference issues in the here-and-now between patient and therapist. Of course, it is possible to misuse an emphasis on transference to collude with a patient's resistance to extratransference material, but it is far more likely that the transference itself will be resisted. The patient is often only too happy to seize on some current problem outside the analysis to evade the immediate, affect-laden issues in the transference. When seeking the transference significance of an external event, it is important not to devalue the importance of the event itself in interpreting its possible relevance for the transference in its appearance in the patient's associations.

IS ANY ANALYTIC RESERVE NECESSARY?

With the recognition of the inevitable participation of external events in psychoanalysis proper, in what I am calling psychoanalytic therapy, and in psychoanalytic psychotherapy, a danger has arisen, There are those who conclude that if interaction is inevitable, there is no need to be so worried about its occurrence. After all, it can be analyzed. As I mentioned, Levy and Inderbitzin (1992) examine the aphorism "All is grist for the mill"; that is, interaction just provides another opportunity to further the analysis. But the phrase arose in the context of inadvertent interactions, such as the accidental meeting of patient and analyst outside the analytic situation, perhaps at the elevator, or at a concert where even the spouse may be in evidence, or at the supermarket with the children in tow; or an illness of the analyst; or even a forced termination because of the analyst's relocation. Other examples are the common alteration of the "frame," such as a canceled or missed appointment or the even more fraught situation of whether the patient must take his vacation when the analyst does.

Discussions of this sort of problem are quite common in the literature, but they almost invariably deal with an *inadvertent* interaction. Levy and Inderbitzin warn that there is a growing willingness on the analyst's part to engage in advertent interactions, such as deliberately attending the same social event, where he may freely socialize with an analysand. With the progressive acceptance of the dyadic nature of the analytic situation, that is, even witting interaction of a fairly intimate sort may be blithely undertaken.

Interaction plays a special role in the training analysis of analytic candidates where the line between advertent and inadvertent is less sharply drawn. Should a candidate take a course taught by his analyst, attend a lecture his analyst is likely to attend? The possibilities are endless, of course. I have already referred to an actual incident that occurred some years ago and had important reality consequences: the wife of a training analyst was denied permission to take an extension course she needed to complete an educational program because the course was taught by a candidate analysand of her husband.

Levy and Inderbitzin have emphasized that attention to external events can be used to defend against intrapsychic issues. This is undoubtedly true, but it is equally true that preoccupation with the intrapsychic can be used as a defense against significant external interaction. Levy and Inderbitzin concern themselves primarily with interactions between analyst and analysand outside the analytic situation. I agree that such gross voluntary breaches of analytic reserve outside the analytic situation can make more difficult the analysis of intrapsychic issues. But the kind of interactions I have in mind, which are frequently overlooked, are the often subtle and chronic interactions within the analytic situation. For example, I mean the analyst who thinks of himself as silent but who frequently says "uh-huh" and deals with silences by regularly asking what the analysand is thinking about, even though the analysand knows full well that he is expected to say whatever is on his mind. Major ongoing meanings of the relationship between analyst and analysand may be hidden in such interactions. Again I remind the reader that I have in mind the subjective intrapsychic meanings of these interactions, which can be disclosed only by investigation, however the analyst may have consciously intended them. He may even remain unaware that he is engaging in them. It is incumbent on the analyst to try to be aware of all that passes between himself and the analysand, verbal or otherwise.

With recognition of the inevitable and unceasing interaction between patient and therapist, suggestions are appearing about how action and interpretation can be employed in combination for more effective therapy. Paul Wachtel (1977) was one of the first to advocate such experimentation. More recently Kenneth Frank (1993) has also advocated such an approach. Sometimes a directive, a piece of advice, a suggestion about how to behave in a difficult situation may seem desirable to break an impasse or an obsessional vicious circle. The possible utility of such analyst actions seem much more acceptable with the recognition that interaction is constant anyhow and with attention to the analysis of such interaction. Whether the therapy remains psychoanalytic therapy will depend on the nature of the deliberate interaction and whether its meaning in the transference is analyzed. Once an analytic situation is established so that the two participants are agreed on the centrality of the analysis of interaction, it may be helpful to relax the strictures against interaction for a more effective therapy.

With this change in outlook on deliberate action, the use of pharmacotherapy in combination with psychological therapy has to be reevaluated. Conventional wisdom has it that genuine psychoanalysis and pharmacotherapy are incompatible in principle. But that may not necessarily be so if the significance of prescribing medication is examined for its meaning in the interaction. The expedient of having another therapist prescribe, even if the original therapist is licensed to do so, seems to me a fatuous pretense that the original therapist is not involved. Far more inimical than deliberate interaction is the denial that such interaction is taking place.

SUGGESTION

Psychotherapeutic "contaminants" in psychoanalysis are often called suggestions. In a narrow sense, the term suggestion is used to designate witting, direct suggestion. But I use it more generally, as Freud (1921) did, to mean both witting and unwitting, that is, direct and indirect suggestion.

Freud's failure to recognize the ubiquity of interaction may be seen in his handling of the problem of suggestion. He clearly recognized the suggestion as employed in hypnosis and in its more general usage to mean interpersonal influence. He defined suggestion as ". . . a conviction which is not based upon perception and reasoning, but upon an erotic tie" (p. 128). It follows that the suggestion he felt was a necessary part of the analytic situation is an unobjectionable erotic transference, or, as he put it, an unobjectionable positive transference (in contrast to objectionable erotic transference). I am entitled in Freudian usage to call unobjectionable positive transference a derivative of objectionable erotic transference because, for Freud, all positive interpersonal feeling is a derivative of psychosexuality. Freud also used the term suggestion as equivalent to transference, not in the sense of distortion, but in the sense of influenceability, as in the group of transference neuroses.

Freud (1916–1917) was clearly much concerned about suggestion. He recognized that it could be argued that all the alleged findings of psychoanalysis could be said to be based on suggestion or transference and hence to be the product of the analyst's mind, not the patient's. He thought he had solved the problem by arguing that, while suggestion played a role in leading the patient to trust the analyst (the unobjectionable positive transference) and thus to make the analytic work possible, the influence of suggestion was dissolved by the analysis of transference. It is easily overlooked that he did not recommend that all transference be analyzed, but only the objectionable positive or erotic transference and the negative or hostile transference. As noted, although Freud regarded the unobjectionable transference as a true transference, he also considered it to be realistic and rational. In that sense, it differs from the use of the term transference to mean a distortion.

Should the unobjectionable positive transference also be dissolved by its analysis? I have pointed out that the idea is illogical, but it would be undesirable even if it were possible. It would amount to saying that after an analysis, the analysand should have no affective residue for the analyst. Such an ideal violates the basic interaffectivity of human beings. All human relationships include an ineradicable substratum of affect. In fact, Freud felt that the unobjectionable positive transference was an essential ally in overcoming resistance. I have already pointed out that what seems to be an unobjectionable positive transference may actually conceal a major resistance and not be unobjectionable at all. But if transference is defined, as I define it, as contributed to by both participants, then the unobjectionable positive transference is based not only on those who treated the patient kindly in the past, but on the kindly behavior of the analyst as well.

Grünbaum (1984) has made a great to-do over the idea that the pervasiveness of suggestion in the analytic situation makes any conclusion from that situation suspect. He argues that, therefore, probative research in psychoanalysis can be done only outside the analytic situation. I strongly disagree. First of all, recognizing the ubiquity of interaction, that is, suggestion, the contemporary analyst can analyze suggestion far more systematically and comprehensively than Freud did. Second, analytic data can and should be studied by analysts other than the one who did the analysis. These other analysts, aware of the ubiquity of suggestion and with the greater objectivity they can muster than can the analyst who did the analysis, can do a good, if not entirely irreproachable, job of evaluating the role of suggestion in the analysis.

The matter of suggestion is very important in the issue of what brings about change in analysis. "Transference cure" is an epithet that analysts hurl at one another. It means that a cure allegedly based on the analysis and resolution of the patient's conflicts was in fact the result of some major unanalyzed interaction with the analyst, whether that be absolution, reassurance, penance, or whatever.

I mentioned the recent paper by Nella Guidi (1993), which proposes the concept of an unobjectionable *negative* transference in parallel with the unobjectionable positive transference. The idea makes sense at once. It is reasonable, indeed desirable, for the analysand to object to objectionable behavior on the analyst's part. Of course, what constitutes "objectionable" behavior is another matter!

Before moving to a general discussion of what is curative (often called mutative, that is, bringing about change, perhaps in recognition that a complete "cure" is an impossible ideal) in analysis, I will describe the analytic situation itself in greater detail, but first some discussion of the much argued question of the relationship between psychoanalysis and psychotherapy.

5

Psychoanalysis and Psychotherapy

A recent monograph by Jerome Oremland (1991) with a critical chapter by me details how the analytic situation, including interpretations, is an interactive one. This insight has important implications for the distinction between psychoanalysis and psychotherapy, in the narrow sense, that is, as distinguished from the broad sense, in which psychoanalysis is a form of psychotherapy. Although I have already discussed this topic to some extent in my introduction, I will now elaborate on it.

In the classical psychoanalytic literature a major distinction between psychoanalysis and psychotherapy is that in the former, a one-person situation and psychology are maintained, whereas in the latter they are not. The distinction is, of course, based on a view of the ideal analytic situation, which I have argued is indefensible.

Once again, experience is too brutal to be overlooked. It is now conceded by many classical analysts that the ideal is rarely if ever reachable. It is recognized, for example, that the analytic situation, with its regularity and frequency of sessions and the analyst's close attention, must be experienced by many patients as providing powerful support. The concept of "holding" as a support, as emphasized by Winnicott (1971) and Modell (1990), is often discussed as though the ordinary analytic situation does not often have major supportive meaning. Of course, it may have different meanings as well: while many patients may experience the regularity, frequency, and close attention of sessions as supportive, others may experience these same features as a terrifying insistence on stripping the patient bare.

In any case, it seems to be fairly widely recognized that the ideal is unattainable and that interactive elements enter to a greater or lesser degree into *any* analysis. A major boost for this position has come from the important research of many years headed by Wallerstein (1986).

He and his team found that it was impossible to maintain the ideal. But unfortunately they did not on that account give up the ideal in principle; they concluded, rather, that it was unattainable in practice. They did go so far as to say that the attempt to live up to the ideal could in many instances be destructive and that the therapeutic goal often necessitated the introduction of interactive *contaminants* into the analytic situation. "Contaminants," by the way, is my word and not theirs, although the word was used in this same connection in the title of a panel at a meeting of the American Psychoanalytic Association (Sources and Contaminants of Analytic Data, December, 1990).

My position is different from Wallerstein's. I regard the interaction in every aspect of the psychotherapeutic situation not as a contaminant but as intrinsic to the procedure. I regard the ideal not merely as unattainable in practice but as fallacious in principle. And there follows from this difference a difference as to principle in the distinction between psychoanalysis and psychotherapy.

Wallerstein (1989) suggested that whereas, in the past, I had insisted on a distinction between psychoanalysis and psychotherapy, a change in my views had led to my blurring that distinction, so much so that I have been reviving Franz Alexander's (1956) position in which psychoanalysis and psychotherapy are indeed not clearly distinguished. I have argued against Wallerstein's claim in an exchange of letters with him (*International Journal of Psychoanalysis*, 1991) and indeed have taken the position that it is *he* who is blurring the distinction, whereas I am making it even sharper than I made it before. My argument rests on two grounds: first, on my distinction between seeing the interaction as intrinsic to both processes versus seeing interaction in psychoanalysis as a contaminant of the psychoanalytic situation, and second, on my view of transference as an interaction that is subject to sustained analysis. The first point is another way of stating that Wallerstein sees psychoanalysis as a one-person situation, whereas I see it as two-person as well. The second point is my argument that the *decisive* criterion of psychoanalysis, one intrinsic to that therapy as against its extrinsic features, is that the transference— the patient's experience of the interaction—is analyzed as much as is possible, whereas in psychotherapy it is to a greater or lesser degree *wittingly* left unanalyzed. It is important to note that my apparent equating of transference with the patient's experience of the relationship can be misconstrued to imply that I mean it is based solely on the

immediate interaction. It is, of course, also based on who the participants are, that is, what they bring to the interaction.

I believe that Wallerstein is misled in his evaluation of my views
because I have rejected the extrinsic criteria of frequency of sessions
and the couch as defining psychoanalytic technique. Confusing me
with Alexander because Alexander also rejected these extrinsic criteria as defining psychoanalysis, Wallerstein sees me as blurring
psychotherapy and psychoanalysis. Again, I say it is he who is doing so
because he sees a continuum from psychoanalytic psychotherapy to
psychoanalysis proper, the latter being distinguished from the former
by the fact that interactive elements in the latter are contaminants. He
believes there is a gray area where psychoanalysis and psychotherapy
can be distinguished only arbitrarily. I believe the distinction is sharp
even if only conceptually so. As I have noted, if the intent is to analyze
the interaction as much as is possible, the situation is a psychoanalytic
one; if it is not, the situation is a psychotherapeutic one. Of course, I
must admit that intention is not always easy to determine, but the
principle sharply divides the two modalities. Wallerstein's principle
does not, because it fails to recognize that interaction is ubiquitous.

Of course, as I said before in discussing an infinite regress, if
interaction is ubiquitous, the idea that it can be "resolved" is illogical.
Analysis of interaction is not the same as dissolution of interaction.
Again, interpretation is also an interaction, albeit of a particular kind.

I do propose a distinction between psychoanalysis proper, which
meets both the intrinsic and extrinsic criteria of psychoanalysis, and a
therapeutic procedure that meets the intrinsic criterion but not the
extrinsic criteria. These issues have been discussed in the monograph
by Oremland (1991). He proposes that the procedure that meets the
intrinsic criterion but not the extrinsic criteria of psychoanalysis
proper be called "psychoanalytically oriented psychotherapy," but I
(Gill, 1991) have expressed my objections to doing so and have
suggested the name "psychoanalytic therapy" instead. For me, both
psychoanalytic therapy and psychoanalysis are aimed at establishing a
psychoanalytic situation.

My views of the relationship between psychotherapy and psychoanalysis can have important repercussions on a psychoanalyst's practice. For many reasons, not least because of the expense, the supply of
patients for classical analysis is clearly dwindling. As a result, many
analysts, especially younger ones, are forced to devote a good deal of

their practice to psychotherapy. That can have unfortunate consequences for their practice of both psychotherapy and psychoanalysis. Because they do not practice much psychoanalysis proper, they do not gain adequate experience in doing analysis. Because they consider interaction permissible in psychotherapy but not in analysis, they may find their concepts of each modality influencing the other modality in unfortunate ways. Specifically, they may become too freely interactive in psychoanalysis without pursuing the interpretation of such interaction, and they may become too withdrawn in their psychotherapy, again without interpreting that interaction.

The principle I advocate would lead to the analyst's practicing analytic technique regardless of the external dimensions of the therapy. Of course, the external dimensions must still be taken into account. One might make an interpretation to a patient whom one expected to see the next day that one would not make if one did not expect to see the patient until the next week. But there are also interpretations one would not make even if one were seeing the patient the next day. As Hoffman (personal communication) argues, there is a therapeutic principle that overrides the principle of always and at once making explicit an insight one believes one has reached.

I have dealt with the issue I am describing in the context of "converting" a psychotherapy to a psychoanalysis (Gill, 1988). I claimed that a psychoanalyst should practice only psychoanalysis in the sense in which I define psychoanalytic therapy (Gill, 1984). In the terminology of the present work, I would say that, excepting only a deliberate decision to practice supportive therapy in a particular case, an analyst should always practice psychoanalytic therapy. An important concern I have with my recommendation to use analytic technique with all and sundry is that if it should turn out that the therapy has to be relatively brief, more might have been accomplished for the patient symptomatically with a more supportive technique.

Freud said that the interruption of an analysis is like the interruption of a surgical procedure. That may well be true the way analysis is still often practiced. But I believe that, with the greater attention to transference in the here-and-now that I prescribe, an interruption need mean only that what could have been achieved has been cut short. I realize that much experience and research are required to support this claim.

It is also important to note, as Hoffman (1991; in press-b) emphasizes, that the technique entails risk. A therapist should begin with relatively cautious transference interpretations. A mistake in judgment, abetted by zeal to employ the technique, could mean that a premature or unacceptable interpretation will result in the patient's flight from therapy. I would argue that the occasional mistake is outweighed by what can be accomplished for many with whom it would have been otherwise impossible.

EXTRINSIC FEATURES OF THE PSYCHOANALYTIC SITUATION

I (Gill, 1984) have divided the criteria for the psychotherapeutic situation, using the term in the broad sense of psychotherapy, into extrinsic and intrinsic, a division highlighted because of my wish to argue that the extrinsic criteria of a therapy are not the decisive ones in determining whether the therapy is psychotherapy or psychoanalysis. Under extrinsic criteria, I include frequency, couch or chair, duration of a session, length of treatment, fees, and even the formal training of the therapist.

FREQUENCY

Freud at first saw his patients every weekday, which in central Europe meant six times a week. How did that happen? Perhaps he was following Breuer, who saw Anna O at least six times a week (indeed, often twice a day). Perhaps it was because it was a doctor's custom to see an institutionalized patient every day, as most of the cases reported in *Studies on Hysteria* were. Kardiner (1977) relates that when he came to Freud for analysis, Freud thought he had committed to five people the 30 hours he had available for foreigners who had come to Vienna to work with him, so each would have been scheduled for six sessions a week. He discovered, in fact, that he had committed himself to six people, so he could give only five hours a week to each. Perhaps it was then recognized that five times a week could be adequate. In any case, the current Western work week is five days.

The importance attributed to frequent sessions may be seen in the fact that Freud spoke of the "Monday crust." Ernst Kris (1956) wrote of his uneasiness that he might lose touch with the patient's unconscious if the frequency of sessions were lowered. This point of view, by the way, highlights how analysis was regarded as primarily penetrating to the depths, that is, to the id, as so-called content analysis. Interestingly, Freud (1913) did say that for a treatment well advanced, three times a week might suffice.

What is present practice? Five sessions a week at most, often only four. The International Psychoanalytical Association requires four times a week for training analyses. With the new policy that American institutes not affiliated with the American Psychoanalytic Association can nevertheless apply for membership in the International, the William Alanson White Institute of New York has been faced with a quandary. It requires a minimum of only three times a week for training analyses. Should it change its policy to be eligible for membership in the International? It has decided not to do so. I believe its experience that three times a week can suffice should not be ignored.

I believe analysts generally agree that some people can form a bona fide analytic situation (I will later discuss what that means) at a frequency less than four times a week, while others cannot no matter how frequent the sessions. Obviously, individual variations are crucial. Jules Eisenbud, in discussing a presentation of mine some years ago, remarked on a case in which an analytic situation could be established only if the frequency of sessions was restricted. With frequent sessions, he claimed, the patient felt unbearably invaded.

Clearly, the frequency required to establish an analytic situation is dependent on the analyst and, perhaps even as much, on the patient. The habit of not using analytic technique unless sessions are frequent is so ingrained that I believe we do not know how frequent sessions must be with what kind of patient—and analyst—to make an analytic situation possible. It seems obvious that with more time, more can be done; but Eisenbud's experience suggests that even this truism may not always be true. It is my view that the possibility of establishing an analytic situation exists no matter what the frequency. Again, whether or not it is advisable to attempt to develop an analytic situation in particular circumstances requires much research. Reality circumstances must of course be taken into account, and how much sacrifice a given patient should make in terms of time and money should be that patient's decision, not the analyst's, or at least a decision that they make together. I question an analyst's deciding at the outset that he will not use analytic technique because he believes the therapy can only be brief for practical reasons. After a period of therapy in which the therapist uses analytic technique, the patient may want to move into a full-scale analysis or simply increase the frequency of sessions; I do not believe that the analyst should foreclose these possibilities by deciding in advance what sacrifices the patient must make to permit such developments. Obviously, the sacrifices that have to be made will play their own role in the therapy.

It has not been demonstrated that a frequency of four or five times a week is always necessary for a psychoanalytic situation to be established or to progress. What has become the custom may not be necessary or perhaps even desirable. When Alexander dealt with what he considered undue dependence by reducing frequency, it was decried as a nonanalytic manipulation. But is an insistence on four or five times a week to induce regression not a manipulation? When does a manipulation become nonanalytic? The answer may be, when it is not analyzed.

A change in frequency has a significance very different from the maintenance of a frequency initially established. A decrease or increase of frequency is likely to take on special significance. Even the declaration that one is changing a therapy from psychotherapy to psychoanalysis without any alteration in frequency or position can have an important meaning. For that matter, a declaration after an initial assessment that one will engage in one or the other therapy carries an important meaning, especially to a patient who knows something of the purported difference, even if the frequency and position will be the same with either modality.

Are there some possible disadvantages to a greater frequency? Might it not indeed foster an undesirable dependence in some patients? Is not a certain period during which the patient is given the opportunity to try new patterns of interaction extraanalytically necessary? Is it not possible that a lesser frequency over a longer period of time will be more effective than the same total number of sessions in a shorter time? Is it necessarily true that each additional hour in a week continues to have the same incremental contribution to process? Clinical wisdom has it that a second session in a week adds a great deal to a single session, but is that necessarily true of a third? Of a fourth?

A practical consequence of these considerations may be that more people will be able to afford an analysis. "Managed care" may be more willing to support more extended therapy if the frequency is less. And many more people may be able to finance analysis themselves if the sessions are only once or twice a week.

It has been argued that, even if psychoanalytic therapy is practiced at a lesser frequency, training analyses of candidates should be at the greater frequency. In fact, George Klein (1973) suggested some time ago that the day might come when classical analysis at four or five times a week might be used only for training. Why? Would not such a practice confirm the candidate in the belief that psychoanalysis can be conducted only at the greater frequency? Would it not confirm the belief that the lesser frequency is a second-rate expedient forced by reality constraints? At the very least, greater consideration should be given to reducing frequency once an analysis is underway, including training analyses.

There is much difference of opinion about whether or not psychotherapy should be taught in psychoanalytic institutes. My proposal is that supervision should include psychoanalytic therapy at different frequencies. Such training is more likely to inculcate a basic analytic attitude on the part of the practitioner than is the present distinction between psychoanalysis proper and psychoanalytic psychotherapy as usually practiced.

How does one decide the number of sessions a week to begin therapy? Of course, the question may be decided by financial considerations. I suggest that one be guided by two principles. One is to give the patient as much freedom to choose as possible, but with the initial frequency—including whether it is to be four or five times a week—jointly agreed upon, with the further understanding that it will not necessarily be maintained. The second principle is that, if possible, any changes that are made be based on evidence in the work itself about which patient and therapist are in mutual agreement. On this basis it may be decided to increase or reduce frequency. This same principle has led me to conclude that to begin a therapy by announcing the "fundamental rule" is unwise; it is better if it becomes clear in the course of the work that the more freely the patient can disclose what is in his mind, the better for the therapy.

The same principle applies to the often vexing questions of whether to charge for missed sessions, whether the patient has to take his vacation time the same time the therapist does, and the like. Fixed rules may seem to avoid wrangles, but the wrangles themselves may be valuable in the therapy. Rigidity begets rigidity or pseudocompliance. The therapist is inevitably something of a model for the patient.

THE DURATION OF A SESSION

For a long time, following Freud's lead, 50 minutes was regarded as the appropriate length of time for a session. An hour seems a natural time span, and it seems, or at least used to seem, reasonable for an analyst to leave ten minutes between sessions. There is the phone call to make, the toilet need, but more important, does the analyst not need a moment to catch his breath, to have some sherbet to clear his palate between courses? I am reminded of Hamlet's complaint that his mother got married before the food at his father's funeral rites had grown cold. Greenson (1974) wrote ruefully of "The Decline and Fall of the Fifty-Minute Hour." Many analysts now see patients for 45 minutes with no time between sessions. Obviously, it is a matter of money. An analyst can see only so many patients—eight, ten?—a day. If they see patients for 45 minutes with no break, they can squeeze in another patient or two a day.

Should the duration of a session, however long, be fixed? I think so. If the time is flexible, even if only by five minutes, the room for confusing transference–countertransference enactments seems large. Within the constancy of the analytic frame, as some (Langs, 1979) refer to the extrinsic criteria, even a couple of minutes can loom very large as a catalyst for such enactments. Analysis is complicated enough without adding such a feature. And yet, once again, rigidity should be avoided. The patient may need several moments to compose himself, or a particularly meaningful issue may just have come to light. The analyst's behavior regarding such eventualities may lead to especially important illustrations of the centrality of the analysis of interaction.

The issue of session length became an important one in the work of Lacan (1977). He might dismiss a patient after five minutes. I find this a gross self-indulgence. And how could he maintain a schedule! Did he ever lengthen sessions beyond the usual time? Did he have a usual time? I once spoke to someone who had been analyzed by Lacan and who told me that the most valuable session of the analysis was one in which he had been dismissed after five minutes. I asked him what was so valuable about it, and he had nothing to say.

I once had the experience of being analyzed partly in two-hour sessions. I understand this was also the practice when candidates from Topeka traveled on weekends to Chicago for their training analyses. I myself detected no particular qualitative difference, although I luxuriated in the long block of time. It had transference meaning, of course. I have heard it argued that some patients begin to open up only toward the end of a 50-minute session and that it might therefore be wise to have longer sessions for such people. I am inclined to suspect such patients may begin to open up only toward the end of the session because they know they can soon escape. Such behavior would clearly be a subject for interpretation. To deal with it by lengthening sessions would be a manipulation à la Alexander.

Edmund Bergler (1938) used to have 30-minute sessions. He said he could do in that time as much as he could in a longer session because, instead of waiting, he simply told the patient early on that he was resisting! How clear it becomes that the issue is the *meaning* of the duration, not simply the duration as such. Of course, there is a basic reality factor too. Some minimal time is required to discuss something in any detail.

THE COUCH

The couch, the famous couch! What would cartoonists do without it? It is even more distinctive than the beard on the man in the chair behind the couch. Why did Freud begin to use the couch? Perhaps as a carryover from his days as a hypnotherapist. Hypnosis was, and still is, considered by many to be allied to sleep, and the recumbent posture is more conducive to sleep. Freud (1913), unfortunately, said he could not bear to be gazed at for eight hours a day. I say unfortunately because that remark made it so easy for critics to claim that the use of the couch was only a response to Freud's idiosyncracy. But is the couch really necessary? The usual rationale for the use of the couch is that it promotes access to fantasy: the patient is less distracted. It is also said to be related to the relative immobility of the recumbent posture. Freud (1900) attributed the comparative freedom of access to the unconscious in dreams to the inhibition of movement in sleep: the person is protected against putting impulses into action. Yet another reason often offered for the couch is that the analyst does not want the patient to be guided by the play of emotion on the analyst's face in response to what the patient is saying. Consistent with my general point of view, I would argue that this is one more way of trying to minimize, if not obliterate, the interpersonal nature of the analytic situation. Nor can it accomplish such a purpose. As Freud said with regard to anyone's ability to withhold his or her reaction: "Our secrets ooze out of every pore." An initially obscure sentence by Freud (1913) becomes clear when one understands it as an instance of his failing to recognize the continuing interaction in the analytic situation: "I insist on this procedure [the couch], however, for its purpose and result are to prevent the transference from mingling with the patient's associations imperceptibly, to isolate the transference and to allow it to come forward in due course sharply defined as a resistance" (p. 134).

How much of all of this, then, is rationale for the couch and how much is rationalization? Patients are likely to talk about very intimate matters in psychotherapy. In the transference they may also express wishes for intimate bodily contact with the therapist. Is it easier for them to do so if they do not have to look at the therapist? Or might it be easier if they can see the therapist and see that he or she is not repelled by their wishes? Is it easier for the therapist to encourage, or simply to receive without discouraging, such material from the patient if the patient is lying down? Patients often spontaneously look away from the therapist, even when they are talking about presumably mundane matters. And the couch itself can be used defensively by both participants; it may be a symbolic barrier rendering what is said unreal, even null and void. So the answer is surely different for different patients, different analysts, and different analyst–patient pairs.

Sometimes it is argued that the important role of the couch in facilitating access to deeper material is a reasonable extrapolation from the rare but not unheard of outbreak of a psychosis on moving from chair to couch. I have never seen that happen, but I suspect that in such instances the more subtle signs of psychosis were overlooked and that the manifest outbreak on moving to the couch is a result of the *meaning* of the couch, perhaps permission now to reveal all, or some other dynamic. As is my wont, I believe that what is important is not the couch as such, but the meanings it has. James McLaughlin has described a case in which the couch unconsciously meant a coffin. Many therapists recommend that if psychotic material appears from a patient on a couch, the patient should shift to the chair, so that his more direct connection with the therapist can give him a firmer grasp on reality. But could the move not also mean that the therapist is frightened, with the patient becoming more frightened in turn? I repeat: the important thing is the meaning of the couch. What is important is its meaning for both participants, not just for the patient. Even if certain responses to the couch are well nigh universal, this may still mean that the meaning of the couch, not the couch as such, is responsible for these responses.

But what do I mean by the couch as such? If it is true that restraint on movement facilitates access to deeper material, does that not come under the heading of the couch as such? I think not. It is still the meaning of the couch that matters. This gives me an opportunity to repeat an important generalization. I do not believe that how something is experienced is the only relevant consideration. It is not true that *anything* can mean *anything*. There is material reality as well as psychic reality, as I discussed in my remarks on constructivism. One can understand responses to the couch in terms of either a one-person or two-person psychology. For example, in a one-person psychology: "I will be unable to act on my impulses, so I dare let myself know what they are." And in a two-person psychology: "You have given me permission to tell all," or if the move is from couch to chair, "You think I am too sick for the couch." Obviously, any move from one position to the other will require especially detailed analysis. And, again, there is no necessary dichotomy between the one- and two-person views. Both can be true.

An aspect of the constraints of reality is that certain external arrangements are more likely to be experienced in certain ways than others. The couch, for example, is more likely to be experienced by the patient as infantilizing than sitting up is. But for any particular analysand a particular position can have a meaning opposite from the more usual one.

The couch has important social meanings that are more general than the immediately interpersonal meanings. For many patients—and therapists—the couch is a status symbol. As such, it is easily subject to abuse. I suppose that in analysis with frequent sessions, the couch will continue to be usual, while with less frequent sessions, even if analytic technique as I define it is used, the chair will be more usual. I think the fact that there are such conventional preferences makes the detailed exploration of their meanings all the more important.

Jerome Oremland (1991) has argued that the sitting-up position fosters attention to the two-person situation whereas the lying-down position fosters emphasis on the monadic, intrapsychic structure. I (Gill, 1991) have countered that if this is so, it may well be a self-fulfilling prophecy based on the therapist's expectations.

FEES

There are many complex issues here. Can an analysis be done at a fee lower than usual? Even without any payment? Many analysts are convinced that all or partial payment by a third party interferes with analysis. I give my usual reply: it is the meaning, not only the fact as such, that matters. Such a view opens the door to the argument that any external arrangement is permissible, if only it is analyzed. That is not my view. Not everything is amenable to resolution by interpretation: a low fee for someone who can afford a standard fee is very different from a low fee for someone who cannot. I have done low-fee analysis for patients who could not afford more, with a quid pro quo of permission to tape-record and use the material for research. While I do not claim that the transference–countertransference implications of such an arrangement can be entirely resolved by interpretation, I do believe a genuine analytic situation can develop in such circumstances.

An interesting aspect of the fee in a social context is whether an analyst charges the prevailing fee or less or more. There are surprising differences in how much analysts in the same community charge, with, of course, complex meanings, not only for the patient–analyst relationship, but for collegial relationships as well. Medical analysts usually charge the highest, then psychologists, then social workers.

DURATION OF TREATMENT

Analyses notoriously last many years. They were much briefer in Freud's day, which, by the way, made the injunction not to undertake any major decisions during analysis much more feasible than it is today, when an analysis can last for even a decade or more. Why do they take so long? Is the generally accepted relative passivity of the analyst a factor? Is there some unreasonable ideal of a complete resolution to all conflicts? Can an analysis acquire the quality of an addiction because of its unrecognized supportive function? Or because of a chronic, unrecognized, and hence unanalyzed, transference-countertransference bond? Can the analyst's separation anxiety make it hard to let a patient go? Does our idealization of the analytic process make it impossible for us to admit that there are limits to how much we can accomplish, or even that we have failed? I have seen an unfortunate consequence of an inability to admit limitations of analysis in the continuing recommendation of more analysis for unsuitable candidates, even without considering that a change of analysts should be tried. I once argued, unsuccessfully, that an institute should establish the rule that after five years a change of analysts in training analyses is mandatory.

Freud's (1937a) recommendation that analysts have a period of analysis every five years could only have been made in the context of relatively brief analyses. Otherwise, analysts would be in analysis all the time—perhaps not a bad idea, considering the ubiquity and centrality of countertransference neurosis and how an analyst's psychology changes as he goes through life.

I should make clear that by psychoanalytic therapy I do not mean brief therapy. Psychoanalytic therapy can extend for years, as long as psychoanalysis proper.

PSYCHOANALYSIS PROPER AND PSYCHOANALYTIC THERAPY

There is a widespread belief that an analysis follows a fairly regular sequence of phases. One belief is that it takes time for a transference to ripen, and that only then is it amenable to interpretation. Hyman Muslin and I (Gill and Muslin, 1976) wrote long ago on the early interpretation of transference. Even more time, it is generally believed, is required for the development of a transference neurosis, a concept about which there is still much controversy. I cannot add to what I have already written on the subject (Gill, 1982). I especially emphasized Edward Glover's (1955) view that the transference must be actively pursued. Whether the transference neurosis of a patient with an "oedipal neurosis" and a patient with more severe pathology differ in principle is still a controversial issue. I do believe it has yet to be demonstrated that the development of either transference or a transference neurosis necessarily takes an extended time. The analytic world is still under the influence of Freud's (1913) dictum that the analyst can set the analytic process going but after that it pursues its own course (p. 130). This dictum clearly presumes the monadic conception of analysis.

The rationale for the idea that transference and a transference neurosis develop over an extended period is that these are consequent on regression, and regression requires time. What it is about the analytic situation that brings about regression is relatively little discussed despite the seminal paper over 40 years ago by Ida Macalpine (1950). I submit that one reason that the necessity of regression is taken for granted is that, if the topic were open-mindedly pursued, the analyst's contribution to the interaction would be starkly exposed. To convert what is ego syntonic in the patient to symptomatic status must require not time for regression but intervention on the analyst's part. A recent case report by Owen Renik (1993) demonstrates the point. He had to insist that the patient's life style was a pathological one before the analysis could enter a new phase.

That successively different problems become prominent as a therapy proceeds is evident. Does this necessarily mean that regression, in the sense of movement to progressively earlier periods of a patient's development, is taking place? I think not. It may, however, mean that material increasingly strongly repressed comes to light. While one can think of this as regression, it is at least equally reasonable to think of it as progression in the sense that the patient is able to confront increasingly distressing issues.

Another common belief about the expectable course of an analysis is based on the view that issues framed in bodily terms are the rock bottom of the analytic process and, indeed, of the psyche. Therefore, it is only when these "depths" are reached that a true analytic process has evolved. Since classical analysis sees this framing of psychic conflict in bodily terms as the idiosyncratic and pathognomic sign of genuine analysis, and since it is believed that an extended time is necessary for issues to appear in bodily terms, it follows that psychoanalytic therapy, even as I have distinguished it from psychoanalytic psychotherapy, is unlikely to be considered true analysis. I argue once again that the analyst's view will play a large role in when explicit or implicit evidence of bodily fantasies will be focused on.

I have heard it said that "Gill believes analysis can be done one hour a week sitting up." In a way that's true, but in another it is grossly misleading. It is true that I believe that in many instances genuine analytic work can be done once a week sitting up, but that does not mean that I believe the same thing will happen if a patient is seen once a week sitting up or five times a week on the couch.

What I am struggling against is the rote acceptance of the idea that an analysis can be conducted only with at least four or five sessions a week and on the couch. I am struggling against the rote acceptance of the idea that anything less than four or five times a week and the couch requires a kind of therapy different from proper analysis. I want the frequency to be the least that is compatible with an analytic process for a particular patient so that analysis can be made available to more people. I want the position to be the one most conducive to analytic progress for that particular patient.

It bears repeating that the optimal frequency and position are as much a function of the analyst as of the patient. I don't want the analyst to use frequency and the couch simply on principle rather than on the basis of what the particular patient requires for an analytic process. Admitting that I am perhaps more impatient than many, I remain convinced that a more active stance than many analysts employ would move things along much more quickly. Passivity in the analyst has been mistaken for neutrality. As usual, I emphasize that the analyst must remain alert to the meaning of his activity to the patient, just as he should remain alert to the meaning of his silence to the patient. I cannot repeat too often that the silent analyst is not doing nothing. Omission of what needs to be said is as crucial a matter as what is said.

An illustration: I recently found in a supervision that despite clearly understanding the following point, the supervisee had great difficulty putting this understanding into practice: When something happened that seemed inevitably to have elicited strong feelings in the analysand, although he did not speak of them or barely alluded to them, the analyst would ask what his feelings were instead of pointing out that the analysand was not reporting his feelings. Of course, if the analy sand were to reply that he wasn't aware of any such feelings, the question would point to the discrepancy between the analyst's expectation that the patient would have feelings about the matter at hand and the patients being unaware of any such feelings.

When I inquired as to why the supervisee had such difficulty asking why the feelings weren't reported rather than what the feelings were, he replied that he felt it was his responsibility to elicit what the feelings were. My remark bears on the development of an analytic situation: it must be a cooperative process. Otherwise the analyst may be setting up a chronic transference–countertransference interaction silently understood to be one in which the analyst is to serve as a constant prod, with heaven knows what unconscious meaning to the analysand of being the object of such prodding, not to mention the unconscious meaning to the analyst of being a prod.

I have written (Gill, 1988) that if therapy is undertaken as I have described it, the issue of "converting" a psychotherapy into psychoanalysis appears in a very different light. The common argument that if psychotherapy has been engaged in the patient should be transferred to someone else if an analysis is to be undertaken is based on the idea that the psychotherapy will have so "contaminated" the transference that analysis of the transference is no longer possible. It should be clear from my discussion that I disagree with such a view, since it implies that analysis can be conducted without "contamination," that is, without interaction. My view is also based on the idea that the preceding psychotherapy will have been conducted along the lines of psychoanalytic therapy as I have described it. Thus do I reach the conclusion that has led some colleagues to opine that I really don't understand analysis: a psychoanalyst should be practicing psychoanalysis—or, probably better put, psychoanalytic therapy as I have defined it—all the time.

I would like to call the reader's attention to a thoughtful, searching article by Helmut Thomä of Ulm, Germany, who questions many of the accepted dogmas about analytic training including frequency of sessions, for the candidate's own analysis as well as those he does under supervision.

6

Free Association and the Analytic Process

I will discuss free association in considerable detail because I think the topic lends itself well to consideration of many aspects of the difference between a one-person and a two-person psychology. Free association is likely to be classed as an intrinsic criterion of the psychoanalytic situation, but whether to call it extrinsic or intrinsic sharpens the realization that intrinsic factors can be divided into those for which the therapist is primarily responsible and those for which the patient is primarily responsible. I have called the analysis of the transference an intrinsic factor. It is primarily the therapist's job, whereas free association is primarily the patient's job. But such formulations can be misleading. Everything in an analysis is contributed to by both participants.

THE RULE AS AUTHORITARIAN

Freud called the injunction to free associate the fundamental rule of analysis. The very use of the word "rule" raises the question of whether it implies an authoritarian stance on the therapist's part that would seem antithetical to the therapist's goal of refraining from imposing his wishes or demands on the patient.

The authoritarian character of the rule may be obscured by the fact that it is called *free* association. The phrase free association is actually used in opposition to *directed* association, the technique that preceded free association. In directed association, which also included a pressure technique, Freud would press on the patient's forehead if the patient's associations failed. Failure, in this context, meant that the patient had nothing to say or nothing further to say about what Freud had asked. While pressing the patient's forehead, Freud would instruct the patient to say the first thing that came to mind. Hence, directed association. Freud wrote: "He is not to keep it to himself because he may happen to think it is not what is wanted, not the right thing, or because it would be too disagreeable for him to say it. There is to be no criticism of it, no reticence, either for emotional reasons or because it is judged unimportant" (Breuer and Freud, 1893–1895, p. 270).

Writing about "superego aspects of free association and the fundamental rule," Mark Kanzer (1972) regarded Freud's way of talking about the fundamental rule as a continuing remnant of hypnotic authoritarianism in psychoanalysis. He wrote: " the fundamental rule did not divest itself entirely of pressure techniques and actually mobilized the superego more insidiously by replacing the external figure of the 'infallible' analyst with the responsibilities and conscience of the patient himself" (p. 257). Kanzer quoted Freud as referring to the rule as an "ordinance" (1910a, p. 32) or "pact" (1940, p. 174) that was "inviolable" (1915–1917, p. 115), with the patient "pledged" (1940, p. 174) to "obedience" (1915–1917, p. 287). Though Kanzer believed Freud became more tolerant and realized that violations of the rule were inevitable, he suggested that Freud may have been deceiving himself when he "invoked the higher authority of 'reality' and represented himself as its neutral instrument." As an example, he cited Freud's (1916–1917) telling the Rat Man "it was not within his power to spare him the necessity of reciting the details of the anal torture which obsessed him" (p. 258).

The wisdom of employing the fundamental rule has been questioned by some analysts, their doubts extending from suggestions that it be worded more tentatively all the way to the conclusion that it violates the very freedom that it is allegedly designed to give by imposing a task upon the patient.

Ernst Kris (1956) objected to presenting the fundamental rule as permission rather than obligation. Quoting from a 1951 paper by Margaret Little on countertransference in which she wrote, "We no longer require our patients to tell us everything that is in their minds. On the contrary, we give them permission to do so . . . (Little, 1951, p. 39)," Kris (1956) continued:

> This statement is supposed to describe "the analytic rule" as it is usually worded "nowadays." This shift in emphasis seems to me to have far-reaching consequences for the structure of the analytic situation. It

makes it more *"personal,"* since the analyst who "permits" and does not "require" free association seems to me close to a parent who does not object to misbehavior. Perhaps this explains why in the paper quoted transference and countertransference are treated as fully equivalent phenomena [p. 451, italics added].

Kris's statement implies that an insistence on the fundamental rule is impersonal, while a permissive attitude toward it is "personal." The implication that there is a correct way of saying something that will prevent the patient from experiencing the analyst as intending it personally is a flagrant illustration of the failure to take the patient's psychic reality seriously as well as a denial of the therapist's responsibility for his interventions.

DEFINITION OF FREE ASSOCIATION

There is an important difference of opinion in the literature as to whether free association is to be defined as whatever the patient says on being given the instruction or whether it is to be defined as a particular kind of association characterized by incoherence and obscurity, essentially a "primary process" production. I agree with Samuel Lipton (1982) that a correct statement of Freud's view of free association is that it is whatever the patient says in response to the request to follow the fundamental rule. Freud cannot be quoted directly to this effect, but I believe it is consistent with all that he wrote about free association and the fundamental rule. He cannot be quoted in refutation of the idea that free association is a primary-process flow, which in its most fully developed form is devoid of resistance, because this idea had not been stated in his lifetime and hence did not call for refutation.

I can, however, cite several remarks that are close to the formulation that free association is that which the patient produces in response to the request to follow the fundamental rule. For example, Freud (1925) wrote that "another advantage of the method is that it need never break down. It must theoretically always be possible to have an association, *provided that no conditions are made as to its character"* p. 42, italics added).

DOES IT HAVE TO BE LEARNED?

If free association is whatever the patient produces in response to the request to follow the fundamental rule, it follows that the ability to free associate does not have to be learned. I quote Freud (1990) again: "The adoption of the required attitude of mind toward ideas that seem to emerge 'of their own free will' and the abandonment of the critical function that is normally in operation against them seems to be hard of achievement for some people" (p. 102). But one page later, he wrote: "Nevertheless . . . the adoption of an attitude of uncritical self-observation, is by no means difficult. Most of my patients achieve it after their first instruction." (p. 103).

In contrast to Freud's view that free association does not have to be learned and consistent with the idea that it is a special kind of communication, Dewald, Kanzer, and Loewenstein have all held that free association *is* something which has to be learned. Dewald (1972) is the most explicit. He wrote: "Most patients in analysis learn the technique of free association only gradually, and usually the best examples of effective free association occur in the middle and late phases of analytic treatment (p. 612). Kanzer (1972) wrote: "Free association is not spontaneously acquired, as has often been pointed out, but is a learned process directed toward an acquisition of insight. . . . " (p. 247). And Loewenstein (1963) observed: "Nearly all patients require not only time, but also some analytic work in preparation before acquiring the ability to follow the fundamental rule" (p. 463). Eissler (1963) saw free association as even more difficult to accomplish:

> In the psychoanalytic process "saying everything" includes not only reporting every event past and present, every feeling, impulse, fantasy, but also that which is considered by the patient to be a lie, a falsification, unimportant, unnecessary. In order to reach the point of bringing all this material into analysis certain changes must take place in the patient. Strange as it may seem, to live up to this requirement is one of the most difficult tasks, and it is questionable whether anyone has ever lived up to it completely.

What is my own position on this issue? I recognize that it may take practice to catch fleeting thoughts and that now and again patients will exclude from their associations something clearly in awareness, but these considerations are not in opposition to the idea that free association does not have to be learned. In any case, the operational definition of construing what patients say as their free associations can be distinguished from whether they say everything they are subjectively aware of.

FREUD: AN EXPANDED COMMUNICATION

Freud's view of free association is that it is an *expanded* communication, essentially logical and coherent, but including certain kinds of material ordinarily excluded from conversation. This means that patients report more ideas than they would in ordinary talking, not that their reports are limited to the added ideas. There is a remarkable consistency in the kinds of thoughts that Freud, in a number of places, says patients should include even if they are disinclined to. These thoughts are the apparently trivial, irrelevant, nonsensical, and embarrassing.

In *Studies on Hysteria*, he wrote:

> The account given by the patient sounds as if it were complete and self-contained. But if we examine with a critical eye, the account that the patient has given us without much trouble or resistance we shall quite infallibly discover gaps and imperfections in it. . . . For we make the same demands for logical connection and sufficient motivation in a train of thought, even if it extends into the unconscious from a hysterical patient as we should from a normal individual. It is not within the power of a neurosis to relax these relations. . . . We may thus suspect the presence of. . . . secret motives whenever a breach of this kind in a train of thought is apparent or when the force ascribed by the patient to his motives goes far beyond the normal ["an inadequate explanation"] [Breuer and Freud, 1893–1895, pp. 292–293].

But breaks can be seen as breaks only if they occur in the context of a logical discourse. This means that before the analyst can construe latent meaning, he has to understand manifest meaning. Both participants have the responsibility to see that they are understood by each other and that they understand each other, although the analyst's responsibility is, of course, greater. If the analyst does not understand, he should inquire, and if he sees he has been misunderstood, he should clarify what he meant. Of course a misunderstanding may also reveal something in the transference that needs to be dealt with. In general, if the patient does not have some distorted notion of what free association is, he will explain anything he has reason to feel the analyst may not understand, such as some technical point about his work or a hobby. But if he mistakenly assumes that the analyst understands something of this sort, it falls to the analyst to solicit enough information to enable him to understand the manifest meaning. Of course, such inquiry may have repercussions in the transference. The patient's assumption that the analyst knows some technical or esoteric point can have many meanings in the transference. The patient may, for example, be testing to see if the analyst will pretend to know something the patient has reason to think he or she doesn't know. Likewise, the analyst's failure to inquire may have meaning in the transference-countertransference interaction. The possibilities are endless.

Kris (1956) described free association in much the same way I have. He wrote:

> We have stressed that the analytic process places the patient in a situation of purposefully chosen lack of structure. The very fact that the transitions from one subject to the other are not regulated gives the role of free association its central position. It is a position characterized by a need to remain comprehensible, to inform, to give accounts, to report, or associate to a dream. While the patient is referred to free association, he has to learn to establish in his contact with the analyst at which point that which he says or thinks can be grasped by his silent listener. It is always of crucial significance when we observe that a particular patient tends to lose this contact, that when invited to follow the pressure of thoughts and images, as they impose themselves upon his mind, he retires into soliloquy and mental isolation. Much more familiar is the opposite difficulty, the behavior of the patient who finds it impossible to relinquish control, to yield to the pressure of inner sources or to acknowledge such pressure. In both extremes, and sometimes for the same reasons, analytic therapy seems unworkable. In the first case, regression shows its power by destroying the contact with the analyst. We are faced with the approach of regression as uncontrollable force, loosened by the very requirement of the analytic situation. In the second case, that same danger may exist, but countercathectic energy directed against the threat of dissolution produces absolute resistance to regression [pp. 450–451].

Kris thus described the two contrasting impediments to free association as following from the fact that, in the analytic situation, contact with the analyst must be maintained, thus making it a two-person situation, though he would probably have objected to this way of putting it.

Kris's opinion presents an interesting contrast to the view expressed by Gedo (1981) and Bollas (1987) that periods of apparent soliloquy are inevitable and even desirable.

AN ALTERED STATE OF CONSCIOUSNESS?

I wrote earlier that the couch is considered by some authors to be essential to producing the *analytic* situation in contrast to the *psychotherapeutic* situation. In addition to the reasons already cited, some analysts claim that the couch is necessary to make free association possible and that the state of mind of the patient who is freely associating is different from the ordinary state of mind. If this is true, that is, if free association is an intrinsic criterion for psychoanalysis, a serious question is raised about my claim that analytic technique can be employed even with alteration of the extrinsic criteria, such as use of the couch. I will return to this point.

Freud's discussion of free association implies that the ideas that are included in the expanded communication are not present in ordinary states of mind; they emerge because the relaxation of resistance leads to an altered state of consciousness. He distinguished between the self-observation of someone freely associating and the state of critically reflecting. As to the former, he wrote: "What is in question, evidently, is the establishment of a psychical state which, in its distribution of psychical energy (that is, of mobile attention), bears some analogy to the state before falling asleep—and no doubt also to hypnosis" (Freud, 1900, p. 102).

Bertram Lewin (1954, 1955) distinguished between free association and the situation in which it was employed, that is, the use to which it was put. He suggested that the distinction between solitary free association and association in the analytic situation is the presence of transference in the latter, although resistance (he called it defense in reference to solitary free association) is present in both. In making this distinction, he claimed to be giving the concept of free association a very loose construction. He proceeded to apply dream psychology to the specific employment of free association in the analytic situation and concluded that

> at its core . . . stands Freud's special, tight definition of a condition of calm self observation . . . something which is quite different from reflection without precluding it. . . . Around this nuclear, strictly defined norm, radiate the states of consciousness of all degrees of awakeness and sleepiness . . . and there are insensible transitions toward reveries and dreams in one direction, and, in the other, toward directed, secondarily processed, structured mental work [Lewin, 1955, p. 185].

Lewin's positioning of free association along this continuum emphasizes that verbal associations are a necessary feature of free association. Even if there is also regression to visual and acoustic images, such regression is in the direction of sleep as in the hypnogogic state short of sleep itself. In another paper on a closely related theme, Lewin (1954) described a patient on the couch as in an intermediate state between sleep and wakeful vigilance. Interpretations of wishes stimulated the patient toward wakefulness while interpretations of defense had a lulling effect. I myself doubt it. Any particular interpretation may be experienced as a challenge with an increase in alertness or as a lulling with a decrease in alertness.

Kanzer (1972) proposed a distinction between free association and the fundamental rule that parallels Lewin's distinction between solitary free association and free association in the analytic situation. He wrote: "The superego is manifest in the operations of both free association and the fundamental rule—two mutually influential but not identical aspects of the analytic procedure. . . . The notion that the former is a state of freely wandering thought can be applied only when the requirement that the patient share these thoughts with the analyst through verbalization is left out of account" (p. 247).

The distinction drawn by Lewin and Kanzer implicitly refers to the distinction between a one-person and a two-person psychology. I suggest that a patient who falls into a reverie may be resisting by withdrawing from the analyst. Gross forms of such resistance are drowsiness, falling asleep, and the spontaneous hypnotic states described by Dickes and Papernik (1977). I believe that the analyst's withdrawal from the patient, in turn, may be related to his or her failure to recognize when the patient's withdrawal is a resistance. Indeed, the redefinition of free association as primary process-like with undisguised regressive content may be an aspect of this mutual withdrawal. I noted earlier that some analysts believe such periods of withdrawal are a necessary and desirable aspect of the analytic process. I submit that a more illuminating formulation is that the analytic situation always has operating simultaneously one- and two- person aspects, but that one or the other will be in the foreground at any particular time (Hoffman, 1991).

FREE ASSOCIATION AND RESISTANCE

A patient who associates incoherently may be doing so not simply out of misunderstanding but as mockery. The view that ideal free association produces primary-process material is equivalent to the idea that free association is in principle free of intrapsychic defense. Loewenstein (1963), for example, seemed to adopt such a position in implying that ideal free association would be devoid of any resistance. He wrote: "Although the fundamental rule itself becomes the target of resistances, and although they hamper the flow of free association, resistances are inevitable. . . . The patient's primary process thinking is being reactivated but he communicates it in words, thus imparting to the primary process important characteristics of secondary process thinking" (pp. 468–469). The view that resistance is superadded to ideal free association is, of course, completely contrary to Freud's (1912b) view that resistance accompanies the treatment every step of the way (p. 103). In line with the injunction to interpret resistance before content, it seems clear, as Busch (1993) has emphasized, that resistance to free association should be analyzed, not overcome by exhortation or even questioning. If the analyst feels that material is being withheld, rather than attempting to ferret it out, as is unfortunately often done, he or she should analyze the resistance to expressing it. Freud himself did not always follow his own rule to analyze resistance. Instead he attempted to overcome it by various means, such as guessing at the withheld content, as he did with the Rat Man's difficulty in describing the torture. In "The Question of Lay Analysis," Freud (1926) observed:

You will not find it at all such a simple matter to deduce from what the patient tells you the experiences he has forgotten and the instinctual impulses he has repressed . . . you will be prepared . . . to work over many tons of ore . . . the patient's remarks and associations are only distortions of what you are looking for—allusions, as it were. . . . this material, whether it consists of memories, associations, or dreams, has first to be *interpreted* [p. 219].

A decade earlier, Freud (1916–1917) had written: "Obsessional neurotics understand perfectly how to make the technical rule almost useless by applying their over-conservatism and doubts to it. Patients suffering from anxiety hysteria occasionally succeed in carrying the rule *ad absurdum* by producing only associations which are so remote from what we are in search of that they contribute nothing to the analysis" (p. 289). Freud, be it noted, does not say that such patients do not free associate, but rather that their productions may be almost impossible to work with.

Fenichel (1953) echoed Freud:

The utterances of a patient *obeying the rule* are not simply a reflection of the unconscious that now becomes conscious. The picture is rather one of a struggle between certain unconscious impulses, which undoubtedly reveal themselves relatively more clearly than in ordinary conversations, and certain resistances of the ego, which similarly are unconscious to the subject, or become apparent to him in a distorted form [p. 322, italics added].

Fenichel obviously believed that even a patient obeying the fundamental rule, that is, free associating, evinces resistance. It is with respect to this issue of resistance that one can distinguish between the view that equates free association with a primary process-like production of undisguised and regressive material and the view that regards whatever the patient produces as his free associations. The former view sees ideal free association as devoid of resistance, whereas the latter view, Freud's view, sees what is produced in free association as both demonstrating the ubiquity of resistance and providing the material that helps make possible the recognition and hence interpretation of this resistance. The patient's productions are compromise formations between opposing wishes, one of which is resistive to the other. Freud's own clinical bias, as noted, was toward uncovering "content" rather than dealing with resistance; thus his suggestion that the analyst whose patient claims to be too embarrassed or whatever should remind the patient of the fundamental rule rather than focus on the resistance. Freud's stricture amounts to manipulating the transference rather than interpreting it.

FREE ASSOCIATING AS A PRIMARY-PROCESS PRODUCTION

Dewald (1972), stating most explicitly that free association is a particular kind of production—primary process-like—apparently does not recognize that his view differs from Freud's. With due appreciation for the service Dewald does us in presenting primary data in his book *The Psychoanalytic Process*, and in recognition that I am dealing with a work written over 20 years ago, I must nevertheless say that his description of analysis incorporates throughout a basic misconception of free association. The matter is thoroughly discussed in an excellent review of Dewald's book by Samuel Lipton (1982), from which I quote:

> That Dewald construes free associations as inherently illogical . . . is obvious, I think, to anyone who reads the book, but difficult to document. It is the fact that all through the analysis, the patient speaks in an illogical way. Much of what she says seems like nonsense. This is not because she has any difficulty in thinking, but because she has Dewald's consent, encouragement, and insistence that she speak just that way. The result is that she omits connecting, explanatory, reasonable ideas so consistently that Dewald's notes of the hours are extremely difficult to read carefully. In hour after hour one can make no sense of much of what the patient says [p. 351].
>
> At one point, the patient herself refers to this, stating, "I feel so much like a nervous little girl. I feel just like my own daughter. When she is insecure, she talks to be sure we are tied together. It makes no sense and it's all garbled. Instead of just saying, 'I'm so scared I need you so much,' I have to go on and talk." Dewald then asked (page 184), "What's the feeling of being so scared?" To my mind the question is not clarifying and distracts the patient from the important point of talking nonsense, but in any event, I found nothing in the book indicating that the matter of talking nonsense had been discussed on that occasion or any other [p. 351].

Later, Lipton writes:

> I was able to find one explicit confirmation [that Dewald's conception
> is that "free associations are inherently illogical"]. . . . That there
> should be only one is not surprising because the occasion for it was
> Dewald's explanation of what in his view was his own error. In one
> hour (page 255) the patient was silent for a minute and then made the
> incomprehensible statement, "They thought I had worms." Dewald
> said, "I'm not clear what you mean."
>   To me, Dewald's statement seemed both natural and necessary. It
> seemed obvious that during the silence which had preceded the incom-
> prehensible statement, the patient has suppressed connecting ideas.
> What had already puzzled me was why Dewald had not made a similar
> comment on many, previous similar occasions. However, Dewald
> himself thought that he had made a mistake, and explained in his
> discussion (page 258) that his statement was "Not ideal in that it
> implies that the last association seems to be out of context and therefore
> *suggests that I expect some type of logical meaning,* but at the same time it
> is sufficiently general so that it does not significantly interfere with her
> continuing to recall the important childhood screen experience with
> the worms" [p. 353].

I object to Lipton's suggestion because it asks for clarification of
content instead of focusing on the implied resistance in the process.
Lipton's suggestion is an implicit manipulation. I would have asked
something like, "Do you realize that I could not possibly understand
what you mean? I wonder what it means that you seem not to feel the
need to make yourself clear to me." Of course, that implies a suggestion
too: "I want you to make yourself clear to me." But, again, there is
nothing the analyst says or does which does *not* carry suggestion,
whether explicit or implicit.

It seems unlikely that Dewald (1972) or any other analyst would
explicitly state that free associations should be manifestly illogical, yet
Dewald implied just such a view. He wrote: "The method of free
association . . . results in an *apparently structureless and random flow of
material.* . . . In essence, *the form and content of mental functioning
manifest in an on-going pattern of free association tends to be increasingly
regressive* in the direction of the primary-process mode of thinking, and
hence tends further to foster the process of 'regression in the service of
the ego' (page 612, italics added). Were the regression indeed "in the

service of the ego," the associations could not in general be "apparently structureless and random," unless such apparent attributes were in the service of the ego's resistance.

That Dewald unwittingly enabled the patient to believe that it was all right for her to talk this way from the very beginning may be seen in his report of the very first exchange of the first hour, the beginning of the analysis. The patient asked what she should do if she is pregnant. Dewald replied that it was necessary to understand what was behind the question to see if it had meaning other than the question itself. Yet the meaning of the question itself is obscure on the manifest level, and the analyst makes no attempt to clarify its manifest meaning (p. 21).

An analyst who believes free association should be primary-processlike may thus lead a patient to understand the fundamental rule to mean that he should *not* speak understandably — perhaps even that *only* those thoughts which Freud described as apparently irrelevant, trivial, nonsensical, or embarrassing should be expressed. While at first glance it may seem absurd to say so, this misunderstanding actually leads to the conclusion that ideas which are relevant, important, meaningful, and unembarrassing should be inhibited. For example, Loewenstein (1971) told an anecdote of a patient who said, "I was going to free associate but I'd better tell you what is really on my mind" (p. 100).

ONE-PERSON OR TWO-PERSON OR BOTH?

The ideal of free association as producing primary-process material would make analysis a monologue rather than a dialogue. Yet Freud (1926) explicitly described the analytic situation as a *conversation*.

Of course, Dewald's patient often spoke understandably. Dewald mistakenly assumed that the breaks in logical continuity were the essence of free association. In a sense he was right, because this is how free association differs from ordinary conversation, but the *breaks become significant only in the context of an orderly flow of thoughts.*

Once again, the crux of the matter is whether the analytic situation is a one-person or a two-person situation or both. The analyst's attempt to deny his inevitable participation in the analytic situation is what results in the views I have described — that ideal free association is a primary-process production with no evidence of defense, as expressed in resistance, and with no need to interpret. In such a view, the analytic situation does indeed become a monologue, a one-person psychology. That this is not a figment of my imagination may be seen in the seriously advanced yet preposterous suggestion of the prominent analyst mentioned earlier that the ideal analysis would be one in which the analyst utters not a word for several hundred hours. Of course, probably nobody practices anything remotely approaching such behavior. Common sense in practice supersedes irrational theory. But there are all shades of practice that come close to the analyst's saying nothing. The silent analyst is no myth.

I am reminded of the story of a businessman analysand who responded to the fundamental rule by saying nothing. This silence continued for several weeks without either participant saying anything. Finally the businessman broke his silence: "Maybe you need a partner!" A joke should not have to be explained, but I want to make explicit the latent two-person meaning of the remark in addition to the manifest wish to share in the analyst's easy and lucrative business: analysis is a two-person situation.

DEALING WITH RESISTANCE

What should an analyst do if the patient seems to be failing to deal with something the analyst feels obviously requires exploration? Certainly, he should not accuse the patient of failing to free associate.

An analyst with a one-person view of the analytic situation is likely to complain that the patient is failing to free associate if something has happened, such as an unexpected cancellation or an approaching vacation by either party, that the analyst feels sure the patient must be having important feelings about but which the patient seems to be ignoring. If the analyst complains or in more subtle ways communicates his dissatisfaction, how is the patient to understand this? If the patient has in fact been saying what is in his mind, he can reach only one of two conclusions: either the analyst does not really take seriously the fundamental rule, since apparently he wants a particular topic to be selected for special attention, or else he believes that the patient is withholding associations.

Another not uncommon situation is one in which the analyst

believes that the patient's free associations are trivial and irrelevant. Paradoxically, then, an analyst who complains under such circumstances that the patient is not free associating is saying so *because* what the patient is saying seems to be irrelevant or trivial.

What should an analyst do when confronted with a patient's failure to talk about matters that the analyst suspects are influencing him or when the patient produces associations that seem trivial or irrelevant? In my experience, the analyst tends to proceed on the basis of the conviction that associations are a compromise formation that necessarily contain some hint of what is being defended against. The analyst will thus offer plausible suggestions about how the manifest associations are an implicit reference to what the *analyst* surmises is the resisted topic. Of course, the analyst may discover that the patient has no sense of omitting anything, or even that he regards what he is saying as far from trivial or irrelevant. It seems clear to me that the better thing to do is for the analyst to inquire into the patient's assessment of his associations, then make clear his own assessment, and then examine how their assessments agree or differ.

If dissatisfaction with the patient's associations is ever justified, it is so only if the evidence is clear that the patient is consciously withholding associations. So long as the patient continues to state what is consciously in his mind, he *cannot* be guilty of failing to associate "properly" since the only instruction he is to follow is to say "everything that is in your mind." Even if the patient refuses to follow the fundamental rule, what he does say can be construed operationally as his free associations and subjected to interpretation of latent meanings. But ultimately the work must focus on the reasons for refusing.

ANALYTIC PROCESS IS PROGRESSIVE

If I argue that a patient free associates from the start, is it my belief that there is no change in the patient's associations as an analysis proceeds? Not at all. There are changes, both in form and content. If the analysis is proceeding satisfactorily, the content will in all likelihood include more undisguised transference material. It may relate more openly to bodily interaction, both sexual and aggressive. But I would not describe that by saying that the associations have become more regressive; I would simply say that the patient is able to reveal himself more fully. Resistance, rather than disappearing, becomes related to new contents (Freud, 1912b, p. 103).

The form of the associations, however, remains that of an expanded, essentially coherent communication. In a successful analysis, the patient's mastery improves, so that the form will in fact be *more* coherent and integrated than before. What was previously indicated by breaks in the logic of the manifest account will now be an integral and coherent part of the manifest meaning. From this point of view, the analytic process is progressive not regressive (Arlow, 1975; Gill, 1984).

FREE ASSOCIATION AND TRANSFERENCE

That the transference is a dominating determinant of the patient's associations, whatever the manifest content, is also stated unequivocally by Freud (1925): "We must, however, bear in mind that free association is not really free. The patient remains under the influence of the analytic situation even though he is not directing his mental activities on to a particular subject. We shall be justified in assuming that *nothing will occur to him that has not some reference to that situation*" (pp. 40–41, italics added). I have written elsewhere (Gill, 1979, 1982) that Freud meant the here-and-now analyst–analysand relationship in this remark about the "analytic situation." Even if one holds that the purpose of analyzing the transference is ultimately to make genetic reconstructions, that goal can be reached only after detailed painstaking analysis of layers of derivatives expressed in terms of the immediate situation.

Many contemporary analysts wait for the transference to be expressed without disguise and even in regressive form rather than interpret its presenting derivatives from clues in content not manifestly about transference. This is especially noteworthy early in analysis (Gill and Muslin, 1976) but holds throughout. The analyst who waits for the transference to become spontaneously and undisguisedly regressive is likely to take the failure of such a development to mean that the patient is failing to free associate properly. In fact, I believe such dissatisfaction may often lie concealed in the definition of proper free association as approaching a primary-process production.

The analyst's presentation of the fundamental rule may of course often become the focal point of important transference manifestations. The analyst may be seen as making an authoritarian demand, a demand that may be conceptualized by the patient on any of the psychosexual levels or their derivatives. Patients will seize upon the fundamental rule as the external reality that purportedly justifies their (transference) feelings. The analyst should deal with these feelings by interpretation rather than by either relaxing the fundamental rule or rigidly insisting on adherence to it.

I have proposed elsewhere (Gill, 1982) that rather than being a spontaneous production from the patient, transference is a joint production of the two participants in the analytic situation. I believe the same revised definition should be applied to the patient's associations. Freud (1925) summarized the advantages of invoking the fundamental rule thusly:

> It exposes the patient to the least possible amount of compulsion [note the implication that some compulsion is inevitable], it never allows of contact being lost with the actual current situation [does he mean the analytic situation, the current life situation, or both?], it guarantees to a great extent that no factor in the structure of the neurosis will be overlooked and that nothing [here he reverses himself on inevitability of compulsion] will be introduced into it by the expectations of the analyst [p. 41].

It is the latter claim which needs to be revised. The very existence of the analytic situation makes the analyst a coparticipant in the patient's associations.

The analyst inevitably influences the patient's flow of associations by everything he or she says and does. Freud's statement that free associations are not literally free does not say the same thing, for Freud meant that there are determining themes within the patient, whereas I am referring to the combined influence of analysand and analyst. The patient's associations in the analytic conversation alternate between free and directed association, in the sense that "free" association usually means that the immediate contribution by the analyst is less readily apparent while "directed" association means that the analyst's contribution is usually more readily apparent; in both instances I naturally refer to what is *manifestly* apparent.

With every intervention, the analyst more obviously influences the associational flow. The intervention focuses the patient's attention on something in his associations with the expectation that he will respond to the intervention. Every interruption of the "free" association means that the analyst loses the opportunity to see where the patient would have gone "spontaneously." But interventions are necessary to convey to the patient the analyst's hypotheses about the latent meaning of his associations. Thus, every intervention by the analyst represents a decision that the advantage to be gained by a possibly correct understanding of an implicit meaning outweighs the disadvantage of interrupting the "free" associational flow that might have further clarified the latent meaning.

What the analyst does after the patient responds to the intervention depends on the nature of the response. He may well conclude that whatever advantage lies in his intervention has been gained, and he resumes listening. The patient may continue to focus on what the intervention was about, but, if the analyst continues to listen, the patient will sooner or later begin to diverge from the manifest direction set by the analyst, at least insofar as the patient's manifest production is concerned.

The analytic conversation, then, is a sequence of free associations in which the analyst's influence is usually less obviously apparent, is interrupted by directed associations in response to interventions in which the analyst's influence is usually more obviously apparent, and then is resumed. Every time the analyst makes an interpretation he further risks imposing his own ideas on the patient. His principal concern in listening to the associations following an interpretation should thus be to evaluate them, that is, to see whether the content of his interpretation seems confirmed or disconfirmed by, or even irrelevant to, the patient's concerns; he must likewise be attentive to the interpersonal impact of the interpretation. It is this close attention to the patient's response to his interventions that makes a genuine conversation or dialogue out of the analytic situation rather than a series of alternating monologues, quite apart from who talks how much.

In referring to the analytic process as a conversation, I do not mean to imply that the roles of the two participants are symmetrical as in an ordinary conversation. Rather, as Freud (1926) put it, the analyst . . . keeps at a distance from the patient, speaking humanly, and surrounds himself with some degree of reserve. . . . " (p. 225). I remarked earlier that Lipton (1977) pointed out that if the analyst is silent it should be only because he is listening, not because he is using silence as a technique. To do the latter is to ask the patient to engage in a monologue. Of course, the analyst's silence may mean many things to a patient. What we hope is that it will mean: "Go ahead. I'm listening." This is a suggestion in a very general sense, since it implies that the analyst wants the patient to say what is on his mind. It may be thought that I am here unduly stretching the concept of suggestion. I think not. I argue that any action, including silence, between two people has aspects of both content and suggestion.

I am thus advocating the kind of freer interaction that Freud engaged in while simultaneously insisting that any effects of such freer interaction which the patient resists making explicit should be interpreted as far as possible. By "as far as possible," I mean as far as the analyst is aware of it and as far as he or she considers the patient able usefully to hear the interpretation.

IS FREE ASSOCIATION NECESSARY?

The question may be asked, then, whether free association is in fact a necessary part of technique. It should be clear that this is not the same question as whether the patient should be given the "fundamental rule." The answer lies in whether the logic underlying the use of free association is indeed valid. This logic posits that analysis is an art of interpreting latent meanings, with such meanings held to be compromise formations between wish and defense that simultaneously implicate analyst–analysand interactions. These compromise formations and references to analyst–analysand interactions, so the logic continues, will make up the flow of associations if a patient follows the fundamental rule; clues to hidden meanings will lie especially in those associations which the patient regards as trivial, irrelevant, nonsensical, or embarrassing.

If the patient withholds these clues, it may be possible to divine hidden meanings without them, though presumably it would be more difficult. Since the art of analysis is to interpret these hidden meanings, however deduced, the goal of analysis must entail bringing such meanings to light. As long as one's aim is to bring hidden meanings to light, one is operating according to the purpose of the fundamental rule. To pursue this aim while pretending that one is not doing so because one has not explicitly stated the rule, as those who imagine they can avoid influencing the patient by saying nothing seem to believe, seems to me deviously authoritarian rather than permissive (Parker, 1965).

I recur to Freud's (1925) claim that one of the advantages of invoking the fundamental rule is that "nothing will be introduced into the patient's associations by the expectations of the analyst" (p. 41). It is this claim which needs to be revised. The very existence of the analytic situation makes the analyst a coparticipant in the patient's associations.

I believe the difference between much contemporary technique and Freud's actual technique (not what Freud *wrote* about technique) inevitably leads to a new view of free association. If I may state the matter in somewhat exaggerated terms, the change from Freud's view is to saddle the patient with an impossible and undesirable task that the analyst waits for him to accomplish. The analyst can never be satisfied, and the patient can never be satisfactory. To the extent that the patient does succeed, he withdraws into a solipsistic autistic reverie, divorced from the analyst. This withdrawal is contributed to by both the failure to engage in a conversation and the failure to interpret the transference, or as Apfelbaum (1966) put it, the failure to engage in ego analysis. This state of affairs contrasts sharply with the relationship Freud sought to establish with a patient: a coherent, expanded conversation in which the patient's productions provided clues for interpretations, mainly of the transference, but also involving how the patient had been molded by his past.

FREE ASSOCIATION AND THE EXTERNAL CRITERIA

I hope I have made it plain that I would not begin by proclaiming the fundamental rule, even if it were worded to make it seem like less of a command.

Epstein (1976) suggests there is a "semantic confusion" in the wording of the rule and that it should be worded as a "desirable condition" rather than as a "rule." Such a view fails to see the primary issue at hand—it is a matter of how the patient *experiences* what the analyst says, not simply what the analyst says. I am not thereby suggesting that exactly what the analyst says makes no difference. If the analyst speaks of a rule rather than a desirable condition, the chances that the patient will experience this as a demand are a bit greater in the former than in the latter. But as I have elsewhere observed (Gill, 1992), that is a statistical issue. What matters is the particular patient: one patient may experience the analyst's mention of a "desirable condition" as a Draconic rule, while another may experience it as encouragement to speak freely.

The point is to enable the patient to speak as freely as possible. The pathway to this goal must be worked out as the treatment progresses so that it makes sense in terms of particular issues in the treatment. Free association cannot be forced by a demand. It is not possible to ward off resistance by a prophylactic maneuver. So I would say nothing to begin with except perhaps, "I would like to hear what's on your mind." There will be time enough to say " Apparently you find that matter very difficult to talk about but I believe it might help if we look at why that is so" (not "try to do it anyhow"). Fred Robbins (personal communication) tells of a patient who had been schooled in the importance of speaking freely. On being asked what she was thinking about when she fell silent, she replied: "I'm trying to think of something to tell you that isn't on my mind!" The remark is very like that of Loewenstein's patient who said she was going to free associate but decided she had better say what was on her mind. She had obviously gained the impression that something other than what she was thinking about was wanted, something strange and perhaps impersonal.

But what of the trivial, the nonsensical, and the apparently irrelevant? Can one expect a patient to include such thoughts without some instruction to do so? Are such thoughts necessary as clues to what is being defended against? Do they not assist the analyst in interpreting the resistance?

The answer would seem to lie in one's general perspective on the analytic process. If one conceives of that process as essentially an intrapsychic exploration, one will consider such clues essential. Furthermore, the search for such clues to intrapsychic defenses puts emphasis on interpreting, or at least understanding the patient by penetration to the depths. On the other hand, a perspective such as I hold, that all consequential matters will find their way into the transference and in that form will be susceptible to interpretations in a way that will be more affectively and ego syntonically acceptable by the patient, argues against a need for the special instruction with its attendant danger of making the patient feel coerced.

The search for the trivial, nonsensical, and apparently irrelevant is an aspect of the promotion of an altered state of consciousness to which I referred earlier and to which I objected. So I conclude, as the reader will have expected, that while I object to giving the instruction to free associate, I believe that what is important about any instruction or lack of instruction is what it means to the patient. Regardless of what is said or not said, the work should be conducted in such a way as to enable the patient to speak as freely as possible. My discussion of free association, of course, applies just as much to what I am calling psychoanalytic therapy as to psychoanalysis proper. In current practice, the instruction to free associate is ordinarily not given in psychotherapy and is regularly given in psychoanalysis.

It is noteworthy that in a study of free association by Joseph Lichtenberg and Floyd Galler (1987), of 49 analysts who responded to an inquiry about how they used the fundamental rule, only two replied that "what is important is not the terms in which the rule is given, but the manner in which it is experienced" (pp. 67–68). It is discouraging that so few analysts were explicit about the difference between material and psychic reality.

Interpersonalists, especially Edgar Levenson (1991), speak of an "extended deconstructive inquiry" rather than of free association. I believe they essentially mean the same thing, although both expressions, taken by themselves, imply a one-person perspective. The interpersonalists derive their inspiration for the idea from Harry Stack Sullivan (1953). Evelyne Schwaber's (1992) emphasis on primarily concentrating on exploring the patient's psychic content is expressly declared by her to be a one-person conception.

7

What Analysts Say and Do

WHAT IS MUTATIVE IN THE PSYCHOTHERAPEUTIC SITUATION?

In recent years, there has been a distinct shift in what is considered mutative in the psychotherapeutic situation. Whereas the earlier view was that change should come about only by way of insight and that change based on the relationship was unstable and was pejoratively referred to as a "transference cure," it is now fairly widely accepted that the relationship does indeed play an important role in bringing about change. For quite some time it was recognized that insight had to be *emotional* insight to be effective, but just what makes insight emotional was not clear. It seemed to mean that the transference was experienced with genuine emotion rather than simply coolly and intellectually. But that still did not entail a recognition of the interaction. It meant only that the analysand's displacement of the past onto the present, allegedly distorting the present thereby, was to a significant degree actually believed to be real by the analysand, however much he came to see in time that what he had thought to be real was in fact a distortion. The analyst's role, as in the conservative critique of the blank screen, was to remain calm and realistic, in short, neutral.

With the recognition of the ubiquity of interaction, how is this changed? What happened first was that it was recognized that the analyst did respond, but it was believed that this response could be solely internal and need not appear in an interaction with the analysand (Heimann, 1950). A good deal of emphasis was placed on how the analyst's awareness of his response could give him vital clues as to what the patient was attempting to enact with him. A frequent formulation was that, just as transference had initially been considered an obstacle to analysis and then came to be seen as an indispens-

101

able instrument of analysis (as in the Bible: "the stone which the builders rejected has become the cornerstone"), so too countertransference, once considered an obstacle to analysis, could now be seen as an indispensable instrument. A great danger, of course, is that the analyst, in regarding his feelings as necessarily "put into him" by the analysand, would fail to recognize the contribution from his own personality. This view is in fact a variant of the blank-screen conception of the analyst's role.

The one-person view became radically transformed by the concept of "projective identification," introduced by Melanie Klein (1975). This concept is a mainstay of Kleinian analysis and has progressively come to influence other schools of analysis as well. It is a concept variously defined and found confusing by many. Perhaps the most commonly agreed upon version is that projective identification is an interactive concept; that is, whereas projection is thought of simply as one person ascribing to another what belongs to the first, projective identification also deals with the effect on the person to whom the ascription is made. If the second person is considered simply the recipient of the projection without being further influenced by it, we have, as noted, a variant of the blank-screen concept.

But many authors now deal with the manner in which the projection influences both the first and second persons. A book by Tansey and Burke (1989) is an example of the careful analyses of various possibilities, particularly from the point of view of the therapeutic process. In simple projection, the motive leading the first person to make the projection is considered to be to get rid of something disturbing to the projector and that he therefore wishes to disavow. In projective identification, on the other hand, one possible intent of the projector is to make the second person feel that which the projector is disavowing.

Another interactive motive that has been described is that the projector hopes the second person will deal with the projection in a more mature way than the projector is able to, in other words, that the projector hopes to find a good example in the second person. That motive is clearly related to the therapeutic process. In any case, the projector may identify with the second person's response. Here is one aspect of identification in the concept of projective identification. A common variant is that the projector feels falsely accused of something and projects it onto the second person to get help on how to deal with an unjust accusation by way of the second person's example. Such a motive is, again, clearly related to the therapeutic process.

An elaboration of what is actually a *conservative* critique of the blank screen, which nevertheless gives a greater than usual role to the relationship as mutative, proposes that the analyst is a guide to the patient by virtue of his setting an example of greater maturity and his faith in the patient's potential for growth. This was in effect the point made in a widely acclaimed article by Hans Loewald (1960). There is an interesting point here with regard to Loewald's reputation. Although he is generally regarded as a classical analyst, one would think that the idea of the analyst's serving as a model would be considered a variety of the "transference cure" abjured by classical analysts. Why, then, was the paper widely admired? I believe because it dared to make explicit what analysts were actually doing and explored a facet of the two-person nature of the analytic situation. But at the same time the concept veered dangerously toward the idea that the analyst is indeed a superior being. If the analyst does behave maturely, it is, as Schafer (1983) points out, because he or she is usually under so much less pressure than the analysand. Yet, an analyst who is ever alert to his participation in the process may be under as much, if not more, stress than the patient.

A later effort by an allegedly classical analyst to approach a two-person view of the psychotherapeutic situation is Sandler's (1976) consideration of the analyst's "role responsiveness." The idea is that the analysand exerts pressure on the analyst to engage in the analysand's neurotic relationship patterns and that the analyst willy-nilly does so. How is this different from the concept of countertransference? It differs in that it is regarded as an inevitable aspect of the therapeutic process rather than as an occasional contaminant to which the well-analyzed analyst does not succumb. Sandler also advanced the idea as a phenomenon that can be helpful to the therapeutic process because the patient's neurotic patterns become more vividly exposed and hence subject to review and alteration. The concept would seem to be a step beyond the earlier one in which the analyst does feel what is induced in him by the patient but does not allow these feelings to influence his behavior with the analysand. A truly interactive concept is one in which both parties are contributing to an interaction, not one in which one party is merely responding to the other.

The point is related to a distinction often drawn between two definitions of countertransference. In the narrow definition, the analyst is simply responding to the analysand's transference. In the broader definition, the analyst is not only responding to the analysand's transferences, but is also contributing something that arises from his own personality, that is, is idiosyncratic to himself.

To return to what is mutative in the psychotherapeutic process, I make this by now fairly familiar claim: it is interpersonal experience as well as insight. How the two are related helps flesh out the concept of affective insight. It is insight into an interpersonal experience between analyst and analysand when that interpersonal experience has affective contributions from both participants, with the analyst's contribution generally being more "mature" than the patient's neurotic expectations, but not so distant from the analysand's neurotic expectations as to be unassimilable.

Hoffman (1992b) has described the foregoing as something old in what seems new and something new in what seems old. That is, the new experience is not a complete reversal of the old, nor is it a stereotyped repetition of the old. The very fact that analyst and analysand usually share the same cultural background, says Hoffman, makes the idea of a stunning reversal unlikely, nor, for that matter, could a complete reversal be assimilated. Slow change by degrees would seem the likely course. Here may be one of the secrets of "working through."

One might ask whether the analyst needs to be a paragon of mental health to engage in such mutative interaction. No, but he would have to be someone who is at least somewhat more insightful into himself than the analysand is about himself. Included in the analyst's insight are the conviction that he does indeed make a contribution to the interaction and a familiarity with general patterns of neurotic interaction and with his own idiosyncracies that he learned in his training. Such aspects of insight increase his objectivity in the progressive stages of the clarification of their interaction.

It should be noted, as Schafer (1983) has pointed out, that the analyst in his capacity as analyst is likely to function significantly more maturely than in his other relationships. The analyst does not have to disclose his neurotic reactions to the analysand, although the analyst will unwittingly express some of his reactions in his behavior. It is the analyst's "work ego" (Olinick, 1980) that participates in the process, not his ordinary social ego. Here is some explanation for why analysts who are seriously neurotic in their social relationships seem neverthe-less to be able to do good therapy. Of course, the more neurotic the analyst, the narrower the range of patients with whom he can work effectively. Every analyst, even the least neurotic, has restrictions on whom he or she can work with. An analyst once told me he had a patient who enjoyed aiming a rifle out of a window at children in the street, though he had never shot anyone. This analyst was unable to work with him. Some analysts cannot bear liars, some cannot abide weeping women, and some are revolted by macho men. It is obviously the analyst's responsibility to refer someone he cannot work with elsewhere, but it is often very difficult to admit a limitation in one's professional capacities.

With the recognition that new experience is one of the mutative factors in the psychotherapeutic process, it is possible to go overboard and belittle the role of insight. Furthermore, the new experience does not remain implicit as it often does in ordinary psychotherapy, but becomes explicit in the context of insight. It is true that if one asks an analysand years later what it was that helped, recollections, which are remarkably sparse, will often be of a particular interaction rather than an insightful formulation. Hoffman (1992b) has related an incident in which during termination a patient said, to Hoffman's surprise, that what had helped her the most was a time when he had voiced an opinion on a political matter that was in disagreement with her view. He tells us that he had been hesitant to do so, not only because it seemed to violate the injunction against imposing his values on a patient, but also because she had made it clear that she was conflicted about getting to know anything "personal" about him. This is not necessarily inconsistent with there having been an adequate analysis of the patient's conflict about wanting to know anything about him. It sounds like the obverse of the usual defense in which the patient feels it is impossible to be self-revelatory without some reciprocal informa-tion about the therapist. Leo Stone (1961) also described a patient who wanted to see him as a mirror, that is, as a nonhuman interpreting machine. This is, of course, a somewhat different, albeit allied, meaning of "mirroring" as used by self psychologists.

In one of my own analyses, of which I have the usual skimpy recollection, I was once bold enough to say, "I'll bet I will make more of a contribution to analysis than you have." I almost rolled off the couch when the analyst replied, "I wouldn't be a bit surprised." I must also regretfully report that the exchange was not further analyzed, not in that analysis at any rate. Perhaps if it had, there would have been less need for another analysis!

It is obviously untrue that the ratio of insight to experience is the same for all analyses. Obviously, people differ as to their investments in affect and intellect, so that one or the other will play the more prominent role in their lives and in their analyses. And, of course, this holds for analysts as well as for analysands.

Glover (1931) wrote a fascinating paper on "The Therapeutic Effect of Inexact Interpretation," which bears on the relative roles of the interaction and insight in bringing about change. In addition to his observation of how different lines of interpretation could provide iatrogenic hysterical or obsessional defenses (usually to shore up those already present), he raised the question of the import of the discovery of a new dynamic previously unknown or the discovery that the theory which had informed interpretations came to be considered invalid. Since both eventualities are very likely, it is interesting to see what he concluded. It is that to the extent to which the analyst failed to deal with the unknown mechanism or used a mistaken formulation, any beneficial effect following on these two circumstances was to be regarded as psychotherapeutic and not psychoanalytic! I am reminded of Masson's (1984) outrageous suggestion that Freud denied the reality of childhood sexual abuse to protect his professional reputation even when he knew better, that this falsehood has influenced analysis ever since, and that analysands should be recalled for honest work the way automobiles are recalled for repair if a flaw is discovered in a particular model. Incidentally, Freud never said that childhood seduction never takes place. He only said that he was obviously wrong in concluding that it was well nigh universal in neurosis. And later, Freud (1931) said that even the act of bodily caring for a child and cleansing its genitals could be experienced by the child as a seduction.

I reject Glover's formulation that "mistaken" formulations and the discovery of mechanisms unknown at the time of treatment justify denying that an analysis had taken place. Since mistakes are inevitable and there will always be new dynamics to discover, Glover's formulation implies only that there can never be a complete analysis. But surely that is clear anyway, especially after Freud's (1937a) late paper "Analysis Terminable and Interminable."

A vivid chapter in the history of analytic thought on the subject of experience as a mutative factor comes under the slogan of the "corrective emotional experience," to which I now turn.

THE CORRECTIVE EMOTIONAL EXPERIENCE

The term corrective emotional experience, originated by Franz Alexander (1956) has long been considered with scorn by most psychoanalysts insofar as it is regarded as implying the importation into psychoanalysis of interpersonal suggestion, a technique considered appropriate to psychotherapy but surely not to psychoanalysis. Psychoanalysis, it has long been argued, should produce its effects by intellectual insight alone. I myself said so in a paper in 1954, a view I have since disavowed (Gill, 1984). Because my 1954 paper is still sometimes referred to approvingly in contrast to my later papers, I have remarked that, in the view of some colleagues, it has since then been downhill for me all the way!

Wallerstein (1989), however, points out that in the 1954 paper I defined the corrective emotional experience and ascribed the same importance to it I now do. I allow myself to emphasize that point because, according to Wallerstein, I have consistently maintained that view to the present, despite what he calls my "dramatically" altered view on "the analyst's active contribution to the patient's transference perception and the plausible construction that the patient gives it . . . " (pp. 318–319).

But the psychoanalytic climate has altered a good deal. It is now fairly widely accepted that new beneficent emotional experiences with the analyst also play an important role in bringing about change. The two factors work together. Jacobs (1990) recently wrote:

> Regarded not long ago as the oddest of bedfellows, insight and "corrective" experiences have in fact turned out to be rather intimate partners. They are not, as we were once taught, mutually exclusive processes technically and theoretically worlds apart. They are rather, synergetic forces in treatment, one paving the way for the other, each important, each contributing in essential ways to the therapeutic action of psychoanalysis [p. 454].

What was the reason, then, for the great to-do about Alexander's proposal, and why is it still almost impossible to refer to a "corrective emotional experience" in psychoanalysis without being considered to be abandoning analysis for psychotherapy? As I mentioned, Lipton (1977) has suggested that a period of undue emphasis on the analyst's abstention from interaction, as criticized by Leo Stone (1961), was designed to counteract the influence of Alexander's recommendation of a corrective emotional experience. I believe that is true, but even more important in the reaction against Alexander's proposal is that he introduced at the same time what he called the principle of flexibility. By this he meant what I would call the analyst's conscious and deliberate manipulation—a far more pejorative term than flexibility—of the analytic situation. Such manipulations were of two main sorts. One was the adoption by the analyst of an emotional stance opposite to the one he considered to have been pathogenic in the patient's development. The other was changes in the extrinsic criteria (Gill, 1984) of the analytic situation, most notably reducing the frequency of sessions if the analysand appeared to be becoming overly dependent on the analyst. It is noteworthy that Alexander did not recommend increasing frequency if the patient kept himself aloof from the relationship.

In the hue and cry over Alexander's defection from analysis, a major contribution he was making was lost, for he had recognized the error of regarding the analyst as a blank screen. Alexander (1956) explicitly rejected the blank-screen concept in a criticism of Balint and Balint (1939), even though the Balints rejected it too because they did not regard it as a significant issue. He wrote: "The authors recognize the fact that analysts do not represent blank screens but are perceived by the patients as individuals with their own character traits. Yet they consider this impurity as negligible for the therapeutic process."

I have already described Hoffman's (1983) incisive distinction between conservative and radical critiques of the blank-screen concept, radical critiques being those which recognize that the analytic situation is interpersonal, or, as Hoffman puts it, social, and which regard the analyst as contributing significantly to the neurotic transference. Alexander seemed to be moving toward a radical critique, but he remained transitional to a full recognition of the social nature of the analytic situation. He wrote that analysts are perceived as individuals (not also that they *are* individuals), and he called the analyst's individuality "an impurity," similar to the term I used earlier, "contamination."

Alexander (1956) argued that the analyst's allegedly blank position is not blank at all: "[T]he objective detachment of the psychoanalyst is itself an adopted, studied attitude and not a spontaneous reaction to the patient" (p. 94). So, he argued, since the analyst is *deliberately* adopting a particular stance anyhow, why not adopt that stance most likely to counter the patient's previous pathogenic experiences? He vividly described how bizarre the usual analytic attitude must seem to an unsophisticated patient.

Alexander's failure was that he did not deal psychoanalytically with his insight into the analytic situation. He became impressed with the ubiquity of interaction, but instead of tackling the problem of how to analyze interaction, he proposed that it be manipulated. Alexander's errors may also be seen in Freud, not only in Freud's failure to analyze the interaction adequately (Gill, 1982), but also in Freud's advice to manipulate the interaction. The latter charge may seem ridiculous to the reader, so let me elaborate.

As I have described, Freud gave as one of the types of transference the unobjectionable positive transference. I have pointed out (Gill, 1982) that the term transference is appropriate for a patient's unobjectionable positive attitude because one criterion of transference is the persistence into the present of interpersonal attitudes based on past experience. I have also argued that all transference is shaped partly by the present situation. This aspect of transference is not readily recognized in the case of an unobjectionable positive transference because the analyst regards the latter attitude as realistic and appropriate.

On further thought, however, it is not so obvious that it is realistic and appropriate. Alexander, as I mentioned, said that the allegedly appropriate analytic stance must strike an unsophisticated person as bizarre. Why should one be willing to trust a stranger who sits behind one and asks one to lie down and tell his most private thoughts while the stranger says very little, if anything at all, and reveals as little as possible of himself? We call the patient's reluctance to do so defensive, but from a nonanalytic perspective, is it not really imprudent to agree trustingly to such conditions?

Of course, Freud (1963) said that the unobjectionable positive transference was based on earlier experiences with someone who was indeed trustworthy, by whom the patient was "accustomed to be treated with kindness." And, of course, it is true that we do not expect patients to speak freely until they have indeed experienced us as trustworthy. Is it not sometimes said that if a patient can truly free-associate, the analysis is over?

But to return to the theme of the corrective emotional experience, I believe that Freud *used* this unobjectionable positive transference rather than analyzing it. How could he analyze it if he regarded its preservation as absolutely essential to the analytic process? He wrote: "What turns the scale in his [the patient's] struggle is not his intellectual insight—which is neither strong enough nor free enough for such an achievement—but simply and solely his relation to the doctor. . . . In the absence of such a transference, or if it is a negative one, the patient would never give a hearing to the doctor and his arguments" (Freud, 1916–1917, p. 445). By the way, an analyst who offers "arguments" is hardly a neutral analyst!

In my monograph on the analysis of transference (Gill, 1982) I argued against Kanzer's implication that, although in the second stage of analytic technique, so named by Freud (1920, p. 18), the analyst used the positive transference to help overcome repression, he abandoned reliance on that aid in the third stage of analytic technique. I argued that, on the contrary, Freud continued to rely on the positive transference, that is, that he did not analyze it (Gill, 1982, p. 155). I can now add an additional piece of evidence to my earlier argument, which I believe strengthens it.

The three stages Freud enumerated were, first, primarily interpretation. In the second, "[t]he chief emphasis lay upon the patient's resistance . . . and inducing him by human influence—this was where suggestion operating as 'transference' played its part—to abandon his resistance" (p. 18). The third stage was that in which the analyst "must get him [the patient] to reexperience some portion of his forgotten life, but must see to it, on the other hand, that the patient retains some degree of aloofness, which will enable him, in spite of everything, to recognize that what appears to be reality is in fact only a reflection of a forgotten past" (p. 19).

Freud (1914a, p. 154) had already called this reexperiencing a transference neurosis, instead of simply an isolated transference, as Kanzer (1966, p. 522) emphasized. This distinction apparently never became vital to Freud, since he seldom used the term "transference neurosis" in this sense thereafter, although his reference in one place to "transference, to give it its shorter name" may mean that he often meant "transference neurosis" even if he spoke of "transference." Kanzer implied that the "human influence," that is, suggestion, of the second stage was supplanted by recognition of the inevitability of the enactment of the transference, which Kanzer labeled "the motor sphere of the transference," taking his cue from Freud (1914a, p. 153). Kanzer (1980) returned to this theme in a paper entitled "Freud's 'Human influence' on the Rat Man." He showed convincingly and in detail that in the analysis of the Rat Man "the need to invoke a special element of 'human influence' to make an interpretation acceptable might have been reduced had the truly vital sphere of interaction between patient and analyst received more direct focus, as in the third phase" (p. 234).

My disagreement with Kanzer is that I believe that Freud never did come to a thorough analytic approach to the problem of "human influence" in the analytic situation. The additional evidence I offer is contained in "Beyond the Pleasure Principle" (Freud, 1920). There Freud added a footnote to his remark that "the repetition compulsion can only express itself after the treatment has gone half-way to meet it and has loosened the repression" (p. 20). The footnote, added in 1923, reads: "I have argued elsewhere [1923c] that what thus comes to the help of the compulsion to repeat is the factor of 'suggestion' in the treatment—that is, the patient's submissiveness to the physician, which has its roots deep in his unconscious parental complex" (p. 20). The reference is to his paper "Remarks on the Theory and Practice of Dream Interpretation," in which he wrote:

> It cannot be doubted that within an analysis far more of the repressed is brought to light in connection with dreams than by any other method . . . there must be some motive power . . . which is better able to lend support to the purpose of analysis during the state of sleep than at other times. What is here in question cannot well be any factor other than the patient's compliance towards the analyst which is derived from his parental complex—in other words, the positive portion of what we call the transference; and in fact in many dreams which recall what has been forgotten and repressed, it is impossible to discover any other unconscious wish to which the motive force for the formation of the dream can be attributed. So that if anyone wishes to maintain that most of the dreams that can be made use of in analysis are obliging

dreams and owe their origin to suggestion nothing can be said against that opinion from the point of view of analytic theory [Freud, 1923, p. 117].

As I described earlier, Freud was clearly anxious about the charge that suggestion brings the findings of analysis into question. In the same paper from which I have just quoted, he also wrote:

The question of the value to be assigned to dreams is intimately related to the other question of their susceptibility to influence from 'suggestion' by the physician. Analysts may at first be alarmed at the mention of this possibility. But on further reflection this alarm will give place to the realization that the influencing of the patient's dreams is no more a blunder on the part of the analyst or disgrace to him than the guiding of the patient's conscious thoughts [pp. 113–114].

Freud reassured analysts by referring to his remarks in the "Introductory Lectures," "where I have dealt with the relation between transference and suggestion and shown how little the trustworthiness of our results is affected by a recognition of the operation of suggestion in our sense" (p. 117). In "Remembering, Repeating, and Working Through" (1914) the unobjectionable positive transference is referred to by other phrases: " a mild and unpronounced positive transference" (p. 151) and "attachment through transference" (p. 153).

The unobjectionable positive transference has been discussed in an important and too little noted paper by Martin Stein (1981). Stein showed the formidable resistances that may lie hidden in an apparently rational, friendly acceptance of the analyst as a trustworthy figure. He emphasized the narcissistic pleasure the analyst may take in being so regarded, which lulls him to sleep and enables him in turn to evade the often unpleasant responsibility of rudely awakening the sleeping patient, to follow him in using Lewin's (1955) metaphor.

I add that this may be a particularly important problem in the training analysis of a "normal" candidate who has especially weighty reasons for conducting himself humbly and admiringly with his analyst, who can make or break him in reality.

With one exception, which I will soon note, Stein dealt admirably with the difficulties in analyzing the unobjectionable positive transference. He criticized Freud's (1913) recommendation that "so long as *the patient's communications and ideas run on without any obstruction, the theme of transference should be left untouched"* (p. 139). Freud found this advice so important that he literally underlined it. Yet it may be precisely in such a situation that the unobjectionable transference operates most powerfully as a defense. The question of the early interpretation of transference is before us. Although I did not adequately recognize the attendant dangers and difficulties, I advocated such early interpretation in a paper some years ago (Gill and Muslin, 1976). In 1969, Brenner had offered the same objection to Freud's dictum.

The point to which I take exception in Stein's (1981) paper is his regarding the interpretation of the unobjectionable positive transference as requiring a special technique:

> I suggest, therefore, that the appearance of the "unobjectionable component" be regarded not only as a welcome manifestation of certain conflict-free psychic elements, but also as the manifest resultant of a complex web of unconscious conflicts . . . their analysis may be facilitated by the use of a process analogous to that employed in the analysis of dreams, particularly with respect to secondary revision [p. 891].

But isn't that process *not* special, but rather how all defensive manifestations are analyzed? What is more likely somewhat special is Stein's description of how this early analysis of the unobjectionable positive transference takes its cue from the here-and -now interactions of the analytic situation: "early impressions of the analyst, derived from a host of perceptions, for example, the mode of referral, the initial telephone call, early impressions of appearance and manner, discussions of indications and conditions for the analysis, including hours and fees" (p. 880). These are examples of the analyst's "contribution" to the transference, which I (Gill, 1982) have emphasized. Robert Langs (1979) termed them the "adaptive context" and also emphasized their crucial importance.

They are well illustrated in a case described by Jacobs (1990). The case made no progress until Jacobs began to focus insistently on the details of the here-and-now relationship, such as the patient's looking at his tie, his haircut, or his "unstylish new shoes" (p. 443). Unfortunately, he concluded in his discussion that all this was *preliminary* to the analytic work and that it is required only in special circumstances.

He claimed that his work in the case would make "Gill look like a slow motion Kohutian" (p. 443), by which he meant (personal communication) that his emphasis on the here-and-now relationship with the patient was so preponderant that it would make even me, someone who emphasizes the here-and-now so much, appear to be slow in analyzing it compared with Kohut, who advised withholding selfobject transference interpretations for quite some time and was therefore even slower than I am. Jacobs's astonishment at his own behavior is clearer than the logic of his comparison!

Similarly, Stein (1981) concluded his paper by writing: "Gill (1979) has described some of the difficulties in the tendency to interpret transference by a too-ready resort to early genetic factors rather than by recognizing the immediate context of the analytic situation. We need not go all the way with him in his emphasis on the 'here and now' in the analysis of the transference, to recognize the relevance of his argument" (p. 890). A recent issue of the journal *Psychoanalytic Inquiry* (Marohn and Wolf, 1990) on the corrective emotional experience includes good discussions of the concept.

HOW SHOULD AN ANALYST BEHAVE?

In the classical view of the analyst's neutrality, his behavior should be punctilious, restrained, distant. I am reminded of a rebellious, sardonic criticism I voiced of classical analysts many years ago—not in print, although I taught it often enough! It was stimulated by a paper by Robert Fliess (1954), the son of Freud's early correspondent, Wilhelm Fliess, on the "autopsic encumbrance." The phrase referred to the fact that a medical analyst's first patient was a cadaver in the dissecting room and that, ever after, his favorite patient was a cadaver, someone (something, rather) whom one could cut into without any protest, in short, without any pesky resistance. Fliess's point was that this early experience made the analyst regrettably intolerant of resistance. Well, my sardonic remark, as I rebelled against the "correct" role of the analyst that I had been taught, was that apparently the analyst was supposed to be a cadaver too!

With the change to a two-person view of the psychotherapeutic situation, how should a therapist behave? Of course, in rebellion against the cadaver view, it is possible to go to the other extreme and make the psychoanalytic situation an egalitarian one, that is, one in which the roles of the two participants are equal. In effect, that would be a situation of mutual analysis. I fell prey to that exaggeration and twice attempted a mutual analysis. Once the patient insisted that was the only kind possible, so I tried it; and once the patient was a very skillful and intuitive therapist who had had several bad analytic experiences. Both instances were disastrous, although in the second one, I don't know how much that was due to serious countertransference errors. I had learned what Ferenczi (Dupont, 1988) learned when he tried it. Doubtless, both of us were similarly motivated to try it. I don't think it can work except perhaps in most unusual circumstances. Therapy is an asymmetrical situation, but I think that, in many instances at least, the asymmetry can, and even should, be far less than is usually considered desirable or necessary.

I believe that some classical analysts think my view of the nature of transference stems from a bias toward egalitarianism and an unfortunate application of that bias to the psychoanalytic situation. Indeed, it has been suggested (Blum, 1986) that my view of transference and the psychoanalytic situation can lead to an exploitative conversion of the situation into a folie à deux. Granted. Strong medicine is dangerous. I recall a remark by Anna Freud (1954) in her discussion of Leo Stone's famous 1954 paper on the "widening scope of psychoanalysis." She said that one finds oneself behaving a bit differently with different patients. With one, one may make a joke, while with another one would never think of doing so. But these are dangerous thoughts, she said, implying, I think, that they should not be further pursued. How dangerous it is for an analyst to think that some thoughts are too dangerous to pursue!

It seems, then, that an analyst's behavior should be somewhere between classical reserve and reckless egalitarianism. Where should that be? One thinks of Freud's (1913) remark that he was not prescribing his own approach for everyone because analysts with temperaments different from his might do better with different approaches. One cannot prescribe the same attitude for everyone. Some analysts are by nature more reserved, and others are more spontaneous. It is common knowledge that many analysts grow more spontaneous in the analytic situation as they grow older. For some, this may be throwing off the shackles of a too rigid classical training; for others it may be the product of experience that a more spontaneous expression of themselves leads to better results; and for still others it may be the self-indulgence made possible by the more powerful positions that often come with age.

So, once more, how should the analyst behave? To begin with, he should recognize that he will indeed behave differently with different patients. But instead of trying to bend himself to a uniformity, he should permit a degree of spontaneity, with the idea that he will regularly, from time to time, stand back and assess the transference-countertransference interaction. He may then see reason to change his behavior, but if the change is major and abrupt he will realize that the patient will be taken aback. He will be alert to such puzzlement on the patient's part, and he may even conclude that his shift has been so radical that he should acknowledge it. This raises the issue of self-disclosure, which I will discuss separately.

The analyst will remember that he is always interacting with the patient and that the interaction is so complex and multifaceted that it is fatuous to think he can always be aware of what is going on. The analyst will work toward the establishment of a psychoanalytic situation. And just what is that? It is a situation in which, however they temporarily stray from it, analyst and patient both remain committed to the idea that the proximal goal is to understand the relationship, not only to engage in it, while the distal goal is to understand the patient's psychopathology in the light of the patient's development.

Hoffman (1992b) has asked how the psychoanalytic situation is to be distinguished from a conventional social situation if the analyst may allow himself a degree of spontaneity in response to the patient. He answers that the psychoanalytic situation presupposes that an integral aspect of the analyst's experience is at least some curiosity about the significance of his reactions within the context of the analytic work. As Modell (1990) has emphasized, one aspect of this notion of the relationship as an instrument rather than an end in itself is that it is designed voluntarily to come to an end, sooner or later. Of course, it never really comes to an end. The analyst lives in the analysand ever after. Modell has described the varying kinds of relationships in the analytic situation as constitutive of different levels of reality. I do not believe this formulation is very clarifying. I believe, rather, that the varying relationships are all compounds of psychic and material reality; they reflect the different underlying assumptions of the participants as to what the relationship is and what it should be.

Indeed, one could simply say that they differ in their transference-countertransference structure. Incidentally, I also believe that Modell's formulation lacks the necessary constructivist underpinning.

The training analysis presents an interesting problem in this connection. Its context is different from that of an ordinary analysis because the analysand can look forward to a continuing relationship with his or her analyst after the analysis is over, even if only on a professional basis. It seems to me that this may be one reason many analysts seem inadequately sensitive to what a powerful jolt it is to a patient to realize that this relationship, which has meant so much, will actually simply end, and abruptly at that, and go from three, four, or five times a week to zero. That is one reason why a termination date is set far in advance: much work must be done on the patient's feelings about the impending end of treatment. It is also why some analysts recommend a weaning period with a gradual reduction in frequency.

I once had the experience as an analysand (some time after I had become an analyst) of having my analyst tell me he would for once break his rule and have a social relationship with me after the analysis was over. In retrospect, I realize that the pressure to do so must have come from himself as well as from me. Maybe no damage would have been done if my reaction to the offer had been carefully analyzed, but it was not. I later had reason to regret that failure.

The training context puts a heavy burden on an analysis. An obvious problem is that the candidate may fear that complete disclosure will lead the training analyst to recommend against his qualification. It is commonly said among analysts that the first analysis is for the institute and the second for oneself.

Aside from those of his formulations of the analytic situation that make it a one-person situation, Freud made several remarks that have astonished me in their failure to take seriously how much an analyst may be emotionally involved in the analytic situation. In one he said that if there is a disagreement between patient and analyst as to whether something had been told before, it was always the analyst's memory that was to be trusted (Freud, 1912c, p. 113n). In another he said that if an interpretation was wrong, it was no great matter (Freud, 1937). The failure of subsequent confirming material would result in its dropping out. And in yet another, Freud (1937) said he did not believe he had ever been guilty of forcing an interpretation on a patient! But, as usual, Freud can be quoted to the opposite effect as well. In one of his last papers, Freud (1937) said that a primary obstacle to the analytic process can be the analyst's personality and that, because of the personally dangerous material with which the analyst deals, he should himself have a period of analysis every five years, an injunction that is all too rarely followed. As I said earlier, the length of an analysis now being what it is, that might mean an analyst would be in analysis all the time. But that might have its merits (as well as disadvantages) too!

In determining the analyst's contribution to the analytic process there is not only his personality to be considered but his views about the nature of the human psyche and what is appropriate technique as well. There are, of course, major differences of opinion about these matters among analysts. What is one to do? Schafer (1979) delivered a very interesting talk about this problem to a graduating class of analysts. In his address "On Being an Analyst of One Persuasion or Another," he emphasized how much the analyst should be guided by his continuing experience.

Ferenczi's shifts in technique illustrate well the fallacy of trying to determine *the* correct behavior for an analyst. After a period of more or less classical analysis, apparently having concluded that the implicit gratifications of the analytic situation drained off the expression of instinctual wishes, he attempted to bring such wishes even more vividly into the analysis by limiting instinctual discharge outside the analytic situation through such draconic measures as limiting the frequency of excretion. Evidently, discovering that such a severe limitation of gratification was unbearable both to the patient and to himself, he went to the opposite extreme and engaged in the well-known intimacies that Freud so sorrowfully opposed in his dear friend's experiments.

Aside from abstaining from such obviously unwise behaviors as sexual intimacy, it is impossible to stipulate *the* correct behavior for an analyst. Every analyst behaves as his or her personality and convictions dictate. As Anna Freud (1954) said, the analyst behaves more or less differently in each of his analyses. Whatever his behavior, it will be experienced as both gratifying and forbidding by the analysand. The analyst's task is to be as aware as he can of how he is being experienced and to use that awareness as wisely as he can in conducting the analysis. I owe to Hoffman this last way of putting it; my own inclination was to say that the analyst should make that awareness as explicit as possible. The formulation "as explicit as possible" can be misunderstood as choosing only *one* correct way. That could be true for an abstract ideal of analytic exploration, but an analysis is undertaken primarily for therapy, intense though the analyst's research interests may be.

I am reminded of the furor caused many years ago by a paper by Kurt Eissler (1950), who argued that if one had to choose between symptom relief or further analysis at a particular point, one should choose the latter. I believe that what he meant was that further exploration would lead to a better therapeutic effect in the long run.

A final note about the corrective emotional experience: Alexander overlooked psychic reality in assuming that because he intended a particular way of behaving to be a corrective emotional experience, the patient would necessarily experience his behavior in that way. The patient's experience could have been quite otherwise. Furthermore, one must question how easy it is to determine just what kind of a corrective emotional experience a particular patient requires.

I believe that a basic problem with many analyses is that the analyst, whether out of anxiety or as a product of his training, withholds himself as a person from the analysand. The patient, in turn, out of motives obvious or obscure, withholds himself too.

WILD AND TAME ANALYSIS

One general way in which an analyst determines his general orientation among the different possibilities can be framed in terms of wild and tame analysis. Some years ago, when I was even more enthusiastic about the centrality of the analysis of the here-and-now than I am now, Fred Pine suggested that I was underestimating the importance of reconstruction of the history. "No, Fred," I said. "You think the history is so important because you are a developmental psychologist. It is therefore important to you. What is important to the patient is to be rid of his pain." Recently, Fred asked if he could quote that in an article. I thanked him for discussing it with me first and told him he could if he would add a footnote, to which he gladly agreed. The footnote was to the effect that I now consider what I had said to be something of an exaggeration, although I still believe that the content therapists emphasize is to a significant degree based on their predilections, and that they also respond to subtle cues (on further consideration, I do not believe they are only subtle) from the patient as to the patient's predilections.

The therapist's ideas as to what will emerge during an analysis play a major role in what will indeed emerge. Would an analysis done by a different analyst on the same patient—a comparison impossible in reality of course—have led to the same material? If an analyst makes a significant contribution to the transference, will the transferences be the same in our hypothetical case? Will there be differences, but only minor ones? An indication that such questions have only recently been taken seriously is the current interest in the influence of the analyst's gender on the course of an analysis.

A remark by Freud seems to open the way to an understanding of the significant differences in the analysis of the same patient by different analysts. He said that an analysis need not recapitulate the history of the patient's development. In fact, a major struggle could take place in an analysis about an issue not important in the patient's development. Freud (1912b, p. 104n) used the analogy of a battle in war: A major fight could take place for strategic reasons over an apparently unimportant piece of ground. That did not mean the national treasury was buried there. This remark clearly has implications for my conversation with Fred Pine.

Freud was the first to use the term "wild analysis." He ascribed to it two main features: an ignoring of resistance and an imposition of the analyst's views. Schafer (1985) discussed Klein, Kohut, and me as proposing analytic systems he considered wild. He argued thus: Kleinians make "deep" interpretations without first dealing with defense as manifested in resistance. Kohut makes certain dream interpretations without first reviewing the patient's associations. Gill is too obtrusive in making frequent interventions and insisting on the centrality of the analysis of transference in the here-and-now, that is, in the patient's experience of the current relationship between therapist and patient.

For Schafer, any insistence on pursuing a particular line is said to merit being called "wild." This is to say that the analyst is not neutral in the classical sense. The two features of wild analysis in Freud's description both entail this betrayal of neutrality in the interest of the analyst's own agenda.

As Schafer recognizes, every wild analysis may at the same time be called tame, for every wild analysis puts obstacles in the way of exposing the correct Freudian story. On the other hand, analysts called wild are likely to refer to an analytic approach different from theirs as too tame. I, for example, believe that the failure to deal with what I consider the most pressing and strongly resisted material available to work with, that is, the interaction in the here-and-now, makes an analysis tame. Klein considered that an analysis that failed to penetrate to the primitive fantasies, which she saw as regnant in the personality, was tame. And Kohut believed that an analysis that took sexual and aggressive phenomena as primary failed to recognize such phenomena as derivatives designed to shore up a fragmenting self and was therefore tame.

Every system considers a differing system as too tame in the sense of failing to deal with what truly matters and too wild in the sense of substituting something else for what truly matters. Each system thus believes it has a hold on what is "really" the case, the truth that will be found if only one proceeds correctly and refrains from imposing one's views so that the material emerges spontaneously from the patient. But is such spontaneity really possible? Is the possibility of uninfluenced spontaneity not contradictory to the constructivist concept? Indeed to the generally agreed upon idea that we are all moved by forces of which we are unaware?

Schafer (1983) precipitated a storm in psychoanalysis by calling the life story developed in a psychoanalysis a "narrative" and by arguing that multiple narratives could be, and are, constructed. He was misunderstood to be saying that one narrative is as true as any other narrative. Of course, it is not. But the criteria for what is "truer" differ from the supposedly univocal truths of natural science. The appropriate criteria for psychoanalysis, as Schafer puts it, are the usually cited coherence, consistency, and comprehensiveness, to which he adds common sense.

Schafer can in fact be read on occasion as equivocal about accepting constructivism. On one hand, he writes, in apparent agreement with Wilburn (1979), of "the intrinsically and fruitfully dialogical intersubjective, coauthored nature of all analytic data" (Schafer, 1985, p. 280). On the other hand, he writes that "the mere fact of interpenetration [a pun on interpretation, implying the coauthored nature of psychoanalytic data] establishes not wildness but the derivation of psychoanalytic meaning through dialogues and mutual influence" (p. 280). The implication is that "psychoanalytic data" are objectively discovered rather than coauthored, even though the discovery comes about by way of "dialogues and mutual influence."

As further evidence that Schafer's embrace of a constructivist position is somewhat less than wholehearted, I cite his discussion of the Freudian analyst's "expertise":

> Freudian analysts view their technical conventions and lines of inter-pretation as expert ways of implementing a necessary and mutative point of view. This expertise is to be brought to bear on the analysand's immediate experience, once this experience is understood, as far as possible, on its own terms. This expertise is to be brought to bear in such a way as to transform this experience *through insight*, particularly through insight into its conflictual infantile aspects [pp. 296–297].

I note again the reliance on the ambivalent and ambiguous phrase "as far as possible on its own terms." And I note further the emphasis on insight, which underestimates new experience, that is, experience of the role of the analyst. Schafer and I finally differ on how much objectivity can be ascribed to the "good enough" analyst. He writes that "the analyst . . . is capable of a noteworthy amount of conflict-free or autonomous functioning" (p. 295). Of course, neither one of us can measure that "amount," so our difference seems to lie in the degree of objectivity we believe the average expectable good-enough analyst can muster.

Narratives in analysis are multiple. Stories change as treatment progresses, not only because different issues lead to different stories, but also because the ever-changing present influences how the past is remembered. With regard to what he calls the Freudian story, Schafer (1983) sometimes seems momentarily to lose sight of his constructiv-ism, as when he writes: "The analyst reconstructs along lines laid down by preexisting theoretical commitments . . . [that] have been worked out, mainly by Freud, so that they fit the material that analysands typically and *spontaneously* (to the extent that that is possible) present in analysis" (p. 204, italics added).

The countervailing tug of the constructivist position is manifest in Schafer's proviso "to the extent that that is possible." For to the extent to which the perceiver influences what he perceives, there can be no fully "spontaneous" data from the patient. What analysands present is also contributed to by the analyst. Schafer recognizes this in his reference to "preexisting theoretical commitments."

To define what is considered a Freudian narrative by classical analysts, I can do no better than quote Schafer again:

> The Freudian analyst . . . progressively organizes this retelling (the revisions of the narrative as the therapy proceeds) around bodily zones, modes and substances, particularly the mouth, anus, and genitalia; and in conjunction with these zones, the modes of swallowing and spitting out, retaining and expelling, intruding and enclosing, and the concrete conceptions of words, feelings, ideas, and events as food, feces, urine, semen, babies, and so on. All of those constituents are given roles in the infantile drama of family life, a drama that is organized around births, losses, illnesses, abuse and neglect, the parents' real and imagined conflicts and sexuality, gender differences, and so on. It is essential that the infantile drama, thus conceived, be shown to be repetitively *introduced by the analysand* into the analytic dialogue, however subtly this may be done, and this is what is accomplished in the interpretive telling of transference and resistance [p. 226, italics added].

Once again, the dilemma of the relation between perceiver and perceived is present. Schafer speaks of the repetitive introduction of the infantile drama by the analysand, minimizing, at least in this formulation, the influence of the analyst on the analysand's experience. Do I mean to imply that a therapist can work without any prior commitments? No. He can only be as alive to them as possible so that he can take them into account. My proposal is not that Schafer is necessarily wrong about the content he expects to find, but that he downplays the role of the therapist's expectations. Further, he may be wrong about the hierarchical relationship between the two kinds of issue he sees as the correct Freudian story, namely, bodily factors on one hand and the infantile drama on the other. Schafer has criticized me for saying that the analytic setup infantilizes the patient; he claims that if the patient experiences it that way, it is the patient's problem. I suggest that his formulation again omits the analyst's contribution to the patient's experience. It is possible, I think even likely, that the patient will plausibly feel that he has been put into an infantile position in relation to the analyst. It will be recalled that Ida Macalpine (1950) referred to the analytic situation as a slow hypnotic induction.

What is especially notable about Schafer's recounting of the Freudian story is not the infantile (childhood) drama, which is considered central in almost all psychoanalytic and psychodynamic theories, but the allegedly progressive organization around "bodily modes, zones, and substances." And so we are led—or should I say I wish to lead!—to psychoanalytic theories of motivation and the role of the body in psychic functioning.

8

Theory and Technique

THE THEORY OF MOTIVATION

Human beings are both organisms and persons. Is psychoanalysis a study of the organism, the person, or both? I believe the lack of clarity on this point is responsible for much of the controversy in psychoanalysis.

One way of approaching the question is to ask whether psychoanalysis is psychology, biology, or both. Obviously the terms psychology and biology can be variously defined. That it is psychology is universally agreed. Whether it is biology too is a subject on which Freud was ambiguous.

Freud's (1905) steadfast insistence on the role of biology in psychoanalysis may be seen in this statement in the preface to the fourth edition of "Three Essays on the Theory of Sexuality," the monograph where he most clearly and comprehensively set forth his early views on sexuality:

> The purely psychological theses and findings of psychoanalysis on the unconscious, repression, conflict as a cause of illness, the advantage accruing from illness, the mechanism of the formation of symptoms, etc., have come to enjoy increasing recognition . . . that part of the theory, however, which lies on the frontiers of biology, and the foundations of which are contained in this little work is still faced with undiminished contradiction. . . . My recollections, as well as a constant re-examination of the material, assure me that this part of the theory is based on equally useful and impartial observation [p. 133].

Why does Freud refer to the *"frontiers* of biology?" And to call himself "impartial" is certainly consistent with the view that he was a positivist, not a constructivist.

On the other hand, there is Freud's (1916) important statement that makes a clear distinction between what is psychology and what is not. It is worth repeating here to show Freud's distinction between biology (organic) and psychology:

> Anything that is observable in mental life may occasionally be described as a mental phenomenon. The question will then be whether the particular mental phenomenon has arisen immediately from somatic, organic and material influences – in which case its investigation will not be part of psychology – or whether it is derived in the first instance from other mental processes, somewhere behind which the series of organic influence begins. It is this latter situation that we have in view when we describe a phenomenon as a mental process and for that reason it is more expedient to clothe our assertion in the form: "the phenomenon has a sense." By "sense" we understand "meaning," "intention," "purpose," and "position in a continuous psychical context" [pp. 60–61].

It is important to emphasize Freud's realization that a mental phenomenon can arise directly from the soma, in which case it is not part of psychology. Only a mental process that is derived from other mental processes is the business of psychology. There is the related and much debated question of the distinction between a drive and a drive representation. Can a drive be a mental phenomenon, or can only a drive representation be one?

Here is a remarkable statement in which Freud (1914b) argues that what he considers a mainstay of classical psychoanalysis – the libido theory – is biology and not psychology:

> I try in general to keep psychology clear from everything that is different in nature from it, even biological lines of thought. For that reason I should like at this point expressly to admit that the hypothesis of separate ego-instincts and sexual instincts (that is to say, the libido theory) rests scarcely at all upon a psychological basis, but derives its principal support from biology. . . . Since we cannot wait for another science to present us with the final conclusions on the theory of the instincts, it is far more to the purpose that we should try to see what light may be thrown upon this basic problem of biology by a synthesis of the *psychological* phenomena" [pp. 78–79].

What is noteworthy about the statement is its ambiguity: libido theory rests "scarcely at all" on psychology and derives "principal support from biology," but then it is psychology he will work with. Of course, the meaning of the word biology can be much widened, as Hartmann did in calling adaptation a biological matter. But I mean biology in the ordinary sense of the body.

The question is this: is it possible for psychoanalysis to be solely a psychological discipline even though humans are not only persons but also biological organisms? Psychoanalysis has a great deal to say about the body. Indeed, many believe that the essential feature of psycho-analysis, that which distinguishes it from all other psychologies, is that sexuality, a major aspect of bodily functioning, is central in psycho-analysis. Why, then, is it that Freud so often refers to psychosexuality, rather than just to sexuality?

DRIVE

A central but ambiguous concept in psychoanalysis is that of drive. The concept of drive as the fundamental origin of the dynamics of the psyche is one of the most disputed issues in psychoanalytic theory. As a theory that lays great stress on bodily need as the driving impetus of psychic life, psychoanalysis must have a bridging concept from the body to the psyche. That concept is the drive, explicitly defined by Freud (1915) as a borderline concept expressing "a demand on the psyche by virtue of its connection with the body." The borderline character of the drive concept is testified to by the arguments about whether it is a biological or a psychological formulation. One facet of the controversy concerns the correct English translation of the German word *Trieb*. It literally means "drive" but in early translations was rendered as "instinct." But the word instinct has the connotation of a more or less rigidly fixed, inborn pattern, which does not accord well with the significant role which learning plays in psychological development. A common compromise translation is the term instinc-tual drive.

It cannot be emphasized too strongly that in classical Freudian theory these alleged instinctual drives are such that they must be abandoned in their original form for development to be normal. They can normally be gratified only in modified, softened, so-called subli-mated forms, a change also often referred to as "taming." The original impulse remains recognizable to some degree, although in some sublimations it can be hard to discern.

Freud (1940) wrote that "the power of the id expresses the true purpose of the individual organism's life" (p. 148). The id, described as a seething cauldron, is metaphorically open at one end to the body and at the other to the psyche. It contains, in some unknown form, the drives, which arise from the body to become psychic phenomena, again in unknown ways. The presumption, however, is that the drives involve energies that, as they enter the psyche from the soma, become psychic energies that seek discharge—this is the central Freudian metapsychological proposition. It is the task of the ego to see that such discharge takes place in ways that attend to the external environment, in ways, that is, which are adaptive. He also wrote: "This concurrent and mutually opposing action of the two basic instincts gives rise to the whole variegation of the phenomena of life" (p. 149).

Freud's (1915) basic paper on the general characteristics of motivation is "Instincts and Their Vicissitudes." He ascribed four characteristics to instincts: source, the somatic process whose stimulus is represented in mental life by the instinctual drives; pressure, that is, the amount of force; aim, in every instance satisfaction that can be attained only by removing the state of stimulation at the source of the instinct; and object, the thing through which the instinct is able to achieve its aim.

David Rapaport (1960), one of the most influential and surely the most systematic of Freudian metapsychologists, also attempted to spell out the general characteristics of the drive concept without reference to the specific content of the drive. He followed Freud in considering an instinct to be a cyclic build-up of energy followed by discharge. He went so far as to say that only drives are motivational causes, while all other causes are nonmotivational. I believe that an implicit reason for his program of defining drive without reference to content was to distinguish between the innate and the experiential. Another reason Rapaport may have defined drive nonspecifically was to distinguish the drives in lower animals from those of man. Instincts in lower animals are highly specific and detailed programs of action, like the nest building of birds, for example; whereas the instinctual drives of man are much less fixed and therefore much more subject to influence by experience, that is, learning (Hartmann, 1948). Such flexibility is a mixed blessing, for while it provides individual opportunity, it also opens the way to individual catastrophe. Freud emphasized that a major characteristic of the libidinal drive is its plasticity or displaceability.

Although Freud regarded drives as the central motivators of psychic life, his theory of drives underwent a number of changes. At first, basing himself on the biological distinction between the survival of the species and the survival of the individual, he proposed two drives, sexual and self-preservative. In a major turn in psychoanalytic theory, he concluded that narcissism – the love of self – was also sexual, and so the drive for self-preservation became part of the sexual drive. For a time the theory seemed monistic. But it became dual again when Freud proposed a death instinct and a derivative aggressive drive relatively late in his career. He said he found it difficult to understand why it had taken him so long to recognize nonerotic aggression. Today, the psychoanalytic theory of motivation remains essentially that of a hierarchy of derivatives from the primary motives of sexuality and aggression, the derivatives progressively taking account of considerations of adaptation to the external world. Freud's theory of instinctual drives is at the heart of his metapsychology. Despite his usual firm adherence to his metapsychology, he also referred to it as a mythology (Freud, 1937a). Central to his work though the metapsychology is, his writings about object relationships are often far from metapsychology. Even in the crucial revision of drive theory in the essay "On Narcissism" (Freud, 1914b), the energy discharge paradigm, as Hoffman (in press-a) has said, is "hanging by a hair."

It is these different aspects of Freud's work which make it possible for many classical analysts to say, in the dispute over the drive and relational theories, that the latter criticize Freudian theory as though it retains the drive-discharge paradigm, whereas "modern (classic) psychoanalysis" no longer does so. The fact of the matter is that while some analysts regarded as classical, like Hans Loewald, in fact are not, the great majority of analysts who adhere to Freud's metapsychology do indeed retain a notion of basic biological drives, even if they soft-pedal the idea of energy discharge.

Freudian ideas about motivation are accompanied by a parallel set of formulations of various kinds of psychic energy; these formulations purport to be explanatory but in my view are, again, only a set of metaphors. They originated with Freud (1895), who began with a description of "free" and "bound" energy in "The Project." Free energy is said to characterize the primary process; bound energy, the secondary process. That energy is free, that is, unbounded, is what Freud says makes possible the primary-process phenomena of displacement and condensation. The concept of libido was also a concept of a particular quality of energy, later to be followed by the duality of "narcissistic libido" and "object directed libido," and, still later, by the complementary notion of aggressive energy.

Freud considered the repetition compulsion and the death instinct to supersede the organism's striving for pleasure, a striving that had hitherto reigned supreme in his theoretical structure. It is for that reason that the monograph introducing the death instinct was called "Beyond the Pleasure Principle" (Freud, 1920). Though Freud originally proposed these ideas as speculative, he later said that they had developed such a hold on him that he could no longer think otherwise.

Far-flung speculations though these ideas are, Freud believed that he had clinical evidence for them. He considered the reliving of traumata in dreams and the reenactment of painful experiences in the psychoanalytic situation to be manifestations of the compulsion to repeat and of its corollary, the death instinct, since these phenomena were contrary to a search for pleasure.

Most psychoanalysts do not accept the concept of a death drive. They hold that its distance from empirical data is such that it can neither be proved nor disproved. The repetition compulsion seems less speculative since it appears to be more directly related to empirical phenomena of repetition; but many analysts believe that repetition, which surely is a major datum of observation, is more reasonably explained by a general tendency to repeat anything that is learned, since learning results in habitual patterns of behavior. Some analysts, self psychologists in particular, distinguish between aggression and hatred. The former is regarded as an adaptive response to attack, while the latter is seen as a maladaptive blind need utterly to destroy an aggressor. Self psychologists term the latter "narcissistic rage."

Freud's paramount position in psychoanalysis is such that much ink is spilt in arguing for and against such grand conceptions, despite the fact that they are far removed from decision by empirical test. Most psychoanalysts—the Kleinian school being an important exception—reject the death instinct but hold fast to the concept of an aggressive drive. Even here there is controversy, however, with many analysts arguing that aggression is always reactive, that is, that there is no innate fund of aggression that demands discharge. The idea that quantities of energy, sexual and aggressive, strive toward discharge is a basic theme in Freudian theorizing. Those who are opposed to this view regard Freud's theorizing on the issue as a reflection of the scientific atmosphere of his time, in which energy and its vicissitudes were the dominant framework of science. This energic framework primarily characterizes the metapsychology, although it has repercussions on the clinical theory.

There have been attempts to substitute an information-theory framework for the energic one, but these formulations seem to me only to replace the energic metaphor with another metaphor that accomplishes the same thing; they add nothing to understanding phenomena in psychological terms.

It was Hartmann who attempted to elaborate the theory of motivation as an aspect of so-called ego psychology, that is, psychology that deals with how the impulses are either defended against or brought to a measure of adaptation and gratification. This was part of his attempt to make psychoanalysis into a more complete general psychology. One of his major proposals was that there exist primary autonomous ego functions, such as sensory and motor apparatuses, that are not derived from the basic drives but are innately present in their own right. Of course, the detailed study of these apparatuses is the province of psychophysiology, studied primarily in academic psychology. Their normal, dynamic psychological study largely comes under the heading of cognitive styles (G. Klein, 1970). A second proposal, now more clearly relating to motive, was of the existence of secondary autonomous motives, which, although originally derived from a compromise between basic drives or their derivatives and the ego, became relatively free of their origin and relatively stable. A third major proposal was that of change of function, in which a motive that developed in connection with one function, defensive for example, came to be employed in another function, such as adaptation.

This expansion of psychoanalysis into what came to be called ego psychology, which is a part of the structural theory of id, ego, and superego, was strongly resisted by some psychoanalysts who feared that the traditional psychoanalytic emphasis on the drives in the id threatened to be overshadowed by ego psychology. Indeed, some critics even proposed that ego psychology was born in a flight from anxiety evoked by primitive impulses in the id. A very common stance taken by psychoanalysts, a rather dubious one in our cultural climate, is that the id drives are so shocking to the uninitiated, and even to trained psychoanalysts, that there is a constant temptation to retreat from, and deny, the underlying brutish, animal aspect of human functioning. It is sometimes argued that the metaphor of the beast to describe Freud's id is an invention of contemporary relational theorists, but was it not Freud who said that the drives have to be "tamed"? Freud argued that psychic illness is one of the prices mankind pays for civilization.

It seems obvious that an instinctual drive must have some bodily source, usually conceived of as a bodily energy, that builds up until it is discharged and then builds up again, thus constituting a cyclic pattern of an innate nature. Such a bodily source seems easy enough to postulate for sexuality by way of the somatic and hormonal sexual apparatus; and, indeed, Freud, in a formulation that he regarded as literal rather than merely metaphoric, saw libido as arising from all parts of the body. But it is more difficult to find such a source for the aggressive drive. The idea that the source of the aggressive drive lies in the musculature has been advanced but has not received wide acceptance. Obviously, one's view of human behavior will be very different if one believes there is a cyclic build-up of sexual and aggressive energies that push toward discharge, in contrast to the view that sexuality and aggression are displayed only in response to an external stimulus. The first view is far more pessimistic about the possibility of the control of sex and aggression than is the latter.

To describe human motivation as sexual and aggressive is to make a very general claim. One wants a more detailed and specified description of the complex web of motivation. To some extent, such specification is provided by the concept of a hierarchy of derivative motivations stemming from the basic sexual and aggressive drives. As I said, such derivatives are described as progressively "tamed" motivations, that is, as more and more reality adapted in contrast to the presumedly wild bases from which they arise.

It is interesting and little noted that Freud (1915) long ago suggested the two contrasting formulations of the relative superordinacy of drive and the self, an issue which is the subject of one of the central disputes in current theory. He wrote:

> Biology teaches that sexuality is not to be put on a par with other functions of the individual; for its purposes go beyond the individual and have as their content the production of new individuals—that is,

the preservation of the species. *It shows, further, that two views, seemingly equally well-founded, may be taken of the relation between the ego and sexuality.* On the one view, the individual [*das Individuum*] is the principal thing, sexuality is one of its activities and sexual satisfaction one of its needs; while on the other view, the individual is a temporary and transient appendage to the quasi-immortal germ-plasm, which is entrusted to him by the process of generation" [p. 125, italics added].

It will be recalled that a major characteristic of a drive is its object. In calling the object the most variable thing about a drive (although paradoxically, he also spoke of "fixation" to an object) Freud clearly made drive superordinate to object. There are two major psychoanalytic theories of motivation that differ from Freud's by reversing the hierarchical relationship of drive and object. One is object relations theory. This theory proceeds from the assumption that man is basically a social animal with attachment to the original caretaker, usually the mother, innately determined. One might think that this theory is only a variant of the classical theory, since attachment could be regarded as a form of sexuality, and especially since the classical view of sexuality is so broad. But I have already mentioned a very important difference. Classical theory considers attachment to the mothering person to be secondary to the gratification of sexual and aggressive drives, whereas object relations theory sees attachment as a primary motivation. The latter theory has been particularly championed by Bowlby (1969), who differentiated the attachment drive into concrete components: clinging, crying, smiling, sucking, and following. Current research on infants appears to be consistent with a primary drive of attachment; it is likened to the clinging of primates (Hermann, 1936).

Object relations—"object" is a peculiarly impersonal term to signify person, but it has currency in the psychoanalytic literature—play a large role in all psychoanalytic theories, whether object relations or drive is considered primary. I mentioned before, but it bears repeating, that the nomenclature of theories in which superordinacy is given to relations among people is confusing. "Object relations" theory is by some considered to have originated with Melanie Klein. She was principally interested in "internal objects" in which the external, experiential relations with these objects was relatively unimportant. For Klein, that is, the relations with the objects were essentially derived from the infant's fantasies. But to many analysts, object relations have come to refer to the so-called British or English school of object relations in which the names of Fairbairn, Winnicott, and Guntrip are prominent. In these theories, much more attention is paid to experiential relations with the object. Confusion in nomenclature results from the fact that the term "object relations" is sometimes used to mean relations among people in a general sense and sometimes in the particular senses of either Kleinian theory or the British object relations school (Kernberg, 1976).

The other main class of theory of relations among people is "interpersonal" theory, founded by Harry Stack Sullivan. This theory is usually considered to deviate much more widely from Freudian theory than the other psychoanalytic theories do. Its deviation from object relations theory is much less than from instinctual drive theory. Its central emphasis is on the current relationship between analyst and analysand. As argued by Greenberg and Mitchell (1983), many object relations theories pay only lip service to the alleged superordinacy of drive. Sullivan (1953) pays far more attention to the infantile drive, called "oral" in classical Freudian nomenclature, than he is usually credited with. He departs from Freudian theory in not regarding this drive as sexual, since he believes that sexuality originates in puberty. George Klein's (1976) distinction between sensuality and sexuality provides a basis for the reconciliation of Freudian and Sullivanian theory insofar as sexuality is concerned.

The primary contemporary home of interpersonal theory is the William Alanson White Institute in New York City. A group of analysts trained in that institute are working toward an integration of Freudian and interpersonal conceptions. They are usually called object-relationists or simply relationists and have recently established a new journal called *Psychoanalytic Dialogues* under the editorship of Stephen Mitchell.

The evidence for psychosexual fantasies, clinical to be sure, seems strong. Whether they play the predominant roles in psychopathology that are often claimed, and whether their regressive revival and modification are indeed the necessary and sufficient basis for the resolution of neuroses, is another matter. Surely issues of uncertainty about one's sex and fear that one is inadequately male or female are omnipresent features of human psychology. The question is whether they are the basic issues from which trouble flows or whether they are facets of more general issues of self-esteem and anxiety about interpersonal relations. One reason it is difficult to decide is that work in the specific area of sexuality may yield results not specific to the idiom in which the work is done but that are effective nonetheless. It is very difficult to question seriously a conceptualization that has been accompanied by therapeutic success. It is also true that so many things are dealt with over the course of an analysis that it is difficult indeed to isolate the central and mutative factors. Reliance on clinical experience alone is very hazardous.

Here is an illustration of the way Freud (1910b) himself could play fast and loose with the word drive: "All his drives [*Triebe*], those of tenderness, gratitude, lustfulness, defiance, and independence, find satisfaction in the single wish *to be his own father*" (p. 173). Similarly, during the same period, Freud conceived of affection as derived from the self-preservative, not from the sexual, instinct (p. 180).

Various classifications of the drives are proposed from time to time, either to supplement or to supplant Freud's sexual and aggressive drives. Gedo and Goldberg (1973) proposed an elaborate hierarchical model of motivation based on progressive maturation. Gedo (1993) later further elaborated this model, culminating in a concept of self-organization quite different from Kohut's theory of the self. Work by Joseph Lichtenberg (1989) is another notable example of a theory of motivation. He proposes five primary groups of motivations: "(1) the need for psychic regulation of physiologic requirements, (2) the need for attachment-affiliation, (3) the need for exploration and assertion, (4) the need to react aversively through antagonism or withdrawal, and (5) the need for sensual enjoyment and sexual excitement" (p. 1).

My reply to Lichtenberg is as follows: 1) the need for psychic regulation of physiologic requirements is not a primary need in the sense of psychology, although disturbances of such physiologic needs can, of course, arise from psychological problems, as in anorexia nervosa; 2) the need for attachment is not a derivative of sexuality in Lichtenberg's classification, while in classical Freudian theory it is; 3) the need for exploration and assertion (reminiscent of White's, 1959, and Greenberg's, 1991, "effectance" motivation) and the need to react aversively are separated by Lichtenberg, while in classical Freudian theory the former is a derivative of the latter. Lichtenberg implies that sexuality is only one form of the broader category of sensuality. As I have noted, George Klein made a similar proposal. Like Gedo,

Lichtenberg suggests that different motives can be regnant in different people.

Although neither Kohut nor his followers have undertaken an explicit revision of the psychoanalytic theory of motivation, they speak of attachment and assertion as distinctly autonomous human motives and even appear to regard disturbances in sexuality as a pathological expression of attachment and hostility as a pathological expression of assertion. These pathological expressions are, in turn, regarded as resulting from disturbances of the self and are considered to be efforts to compensate for the threatened fragmentation of what would normally be a cohesive self. Wishes for mirroring, idealizing, and twinship are implied to be innate motivational strivings.

There are also some psychoanalytic theories of motivation that propose concepts of broad scope akin to Freud's original division of motivation into the sexual and the self-preservative, the survival of the species and of the individual, respectively. Jay Greenberg (1991), for example, divides motives into the broad categories of safety, the survival of the individual, and, as I mentioned, effectance, the freer expression of the individual's capacities. Joseph Sandler (1983; Sandler and Sandler, 1983) has also emphasized the individual's pursuit of safety. Another common division is into the contrasting drives for autonomy and relations with others, or between independence and dependence. Kohut criticized classical theory for considering motivation to be a striving for progressive autonomy from others, because in his view maturity includes a continuing need for others as "mature" selfobjects. Hoffman (in press-a) has criticized Greenberg's attempts to force the psychoanalytic theory of motivation into a single, inclusive, dichotomous pair.

In retrospect, it is a puzzle that affect has not played a more direct role in the psychoanalytic theory of motivation, The relationship between drive and affect has always been close in psychoanalytic theory. Freud called affect one of the two representatives of instinct, idea being the other. Why not affect more directly? If the answer is that Freud found it important to insist on man as a biological organism as well as a person, are not affects even more manifestly bodily than the putative instinctual drives?

Development obviously shows a progressive differentiation of affect coordinate with progressive cognitive development. The psychoanalytic literature has primarily focused on anxiety, depression, and shame. Although there are many articles dealing with specific affects, these have not usually been organized into an encompassing theory of affects. Nevertheless there are several such attempts in our literature. Basch (1976) has developed such a theory, basing himself on the classification of affects proposed by Tomkins (1981). Kernberg (1976), as I mentioned, proposes that the original unit of psychic functioning is an object representation and a self-representation united by a particular affect, at first globally positive or negative. More recently, Charles Spezzano (1993) has written an important monograph on affect as the central motivational concept.

The difference among the several different schools of psychoanalysis lies centrally in their theories of motivation. The classical school regards all motives as derivations of sexuality and aggression, bodily at the root; the various object relations schools, including the interpersonal, regard motivation as centrally the maintenance of patterns of relationships with other people; and self psychology regards motivation as centrally the maintenance of the cohesion of the self. Each school takes more or less account of the central concepts of the other schools, whose concepts are understood in terms of each school's own central concept.

Although the classical psychoanalytic literature, in describing this or that specific motivation, does go beyond broad formulations of sex and aggression, the theory that all motives are derivatives of the two basic drives long stifled any attempt to develop a comprehensive, detailed inventory of motivations, although such efforts are found in the academic psychological literature. Since in practice what the analyst deals with are motivations of a much more specific character than simply sex or aggression, the result is that he has historically been guided by intuitive ideas about human motivation of which he has no formal knowledge. Can psychological sensitivity to the range and permutations of motivations be taught, or has it been decided long before the time of professional training? Roy Schafer's (1976) concept of an "action language," which reconceptualizes motives as actions, seems to me helpful in fostering such sensitivity. It is not only an effort to abolish the reification of alleged instinctual forces pushing the individual, but also an implicit effort to recognize the congeries of motives with which each individual analyst works.

Since first writing this section I have become acquainted with a very interesting volume by Slavin and Kriegman (1992), *The Adaptive*

Design of the Human Psyche. As I read the authors, they return in a sense to Freud's original division of motives between preservation of the self and preservation of the species. Unlike Freud, however, they regard the preservation of the species by way of the sexual drive as a distal motivational cause, the proximal aspect of which is expressed as altruism. Rather than regarding altruism as a defense against hostility, they see both self-preservation and altruism as innate. The conflict between the two is, therefore, both intrapsychic and in relation to the competing self-preservative and altruistic motives of other human beings. Slavin and Kriegman believe that their vision permits an integration of drive and relational theories, although their concept of drive is different from what they see as the reductionist concept of classical drive theory. Their views are worth studying.

In this connection I am reminded that Rapaport's (1957) concept of relative autonomy from drive on one hand and environment on the other implies a related conception. He argued that both drive and relations to the environment, are innate in what he called "apparatus." Each protects the individual against slavery to the other, drive against pathological subservience to the environment, and relations to the environment against subservience to drive. He sketched the pathological consequences of the loss of either type of relative autonomy. On a historical note I might add that one of his related interests at the time of his untimely death was the origin of altruism.

9

The Body in Psychoanalysis

An important context in which a Freudian analyst listens to his patient is in reference to the body, whether explicit or implicit. A common knee-jerk reaction to characterizing psychoanalysis as hermeneutic, in addition to the alleged implication that psychoanalysis cannot be a science, is that the hermeneutic perspective jettisons Freud's great discovery of the role of the body in human psychology. I do not believe that it necessarily does, but the point is not easy to make clear.

In simplest terms, the question is whether it is the body as such or the body in terms of its meanings that is relevant in human psychology. The body as such is the natural science point of view; the body in its meaning to the individual is the hermeneutic point of view.

As a hermeneutic science, psychoanalysis is not all of psychology. I dealt earlier with the effort within so-called ego psychology to make psychoanalysis a general psychology; this effort, I submit, was ill fated. Edelson (1988) has argued that there are psychological functions, like memory and perception, that are—contra Hartmann's autonomous apparatus—not within the domain of psychoanalysis. Such functions can be influenced by wishes, values, and the like and then become of interest to psychoanalysis, but the functions themselves in their somatic structure are not. The deterioration of memory with aging, for example, is not a matter for psychoanalytic study except insofar as the individual reacts to such deterioration in terms of an idiosyncratic way grounded in his personality. Once again, we arrive at the distinction between biology and psychology.

Earlier in this work, I described the innate and the experiential as the grouping of the two factors that must be taken into account in any discussion of psychic functioning. In usual terms, the innate in psychoanalytic theory is the body, but, at least for Slavin and

Kriegman (1992), adaptive relations with the environment have innate roots too. There is even a hint of the latter in Freud's late concept of hereditary elements in the ego as well as in the id. I myself use the concept of the body as a more general term to encompass the sexual and aggressive drives in psychoanalytic theory, now shorn of the specific classical, physicochemical, Freudian metapsychology.

That sexuality has innate roots in the body is obvious. Whether or not there is an innate fund of aggressive energy that demands discharge is a debated point. In any case, the capacity to express aggression is innate.

Psychoanalytic theory is more inclined to discuss the innate in terms of sexuality rather than of the body more generally. Freudian analysts regard their view of sexuality in general and infantile sexuality in particular as what separates analysis from all other systems of psychology. While the Freudian view of sexuality is often misunderstood, it remains true that sexuality is accorded a basic and overriding importance in Freudian theory. Freudianism has been castigated as a perverse, even obscene, doctrine. Freudians maintain that their view of sexuality is far broader than the conventional view. This broader conception may be considered in two aspects. One is that Freudians do not conceive of sexuality in simple bodily terms but rather as "psychosexuality," that is, as a complex amalgam of bodily features and psychological attitudes. There are passages in which Freud explicitly equates sexuality with the very broad concept of love. On the other hand, another way in which the Freudian concept of sexuality is extended is in the view that sexuality begins with the beginning of life and goes through several pregenital stages. Though the claim was disputed by Sulloway (1983), Freudians and others have long held that both the empirical discovery and the conceptual systematization of infantile sexuality are among Freud's greatest achievements. Freud proposed the well-known epigenetic—that is, constitutionally determined—developmental sequence of sexuality's beginning from birth and moving, according to the successively dominant bodily zones, through the oral, anal, phallic, and genital phases. These psychosexual stages are primarily conceived of as the discharge of a particular kind of libidinal energy. While the discharge takes place in relation to an object, this object need not be a person nor even a part of the external world, except insofar as the subject's own body, which may be the object, is considered part of the external world. The first three psychosexual stages constitute the period up to about the age of five, which is the time of the famous Oedipus complex. From that time until a resurgence of sexuality at the time of puberty, there is considered to be, with many variations in degree, a period of latency, a quiescence of sexuality in its more bodily expressions and its "sublimation" into social and educational activities.

It is important to be clear about the distinction between metaphoric expression of the material bodily zones with their modes and substances and metaphoric expression of the ideas of these zones with their modes and substances. In the former there is often an actual bodily manifestation, for example, withholding of feces; this bodily manifestation, in turn, may be a metaphoric expression of a personality trait of stinginess. On the other hand, stinginess may be expressed by the withholding of ideas, with the mind conceived of as a bowel and ideas as feces. This is again a metaphor but one expressed in ideation rather than somatically. These two kinds of metaphoric expression of stinginess, one in bodily activity and the other in mental activity, are often confused both in classical psychoanalytic thought and among critics of the classical viewpoint. A fantasy of the mind as a body in which the mind is conceived of as ingesting, excreting, impregnating, or whatever should not be mistaken for actual bodily functioning.

Classical analysts are alert to evidence of such expression of fantasies and character traits, both by way of actual bodily functioning and by way of ideation about the body, and give them special importance in clinical work. But analysts are prone to the common error of regarding metaphoric mental functioning in which the metaphor is expressed in bodily terms as *necessarily* a derivative of material bodily functioning. A secretiveness about one's thoughts is not necessarily a metaphor for anal withholding, for example. Nor is a woman's penis envy necessarily a concrete wish for a penis; it may be a metaphor for male prerogatives. Nor is a desire for male prerogatives necessarily a metaphor derived from a material wish for a penis. Obviously, penis envy can be both material and metaphorical. In classical analysis, if stinginess and anal withholding occur together, the stinginess is likely to be seen as a metaphor for anal withholding rather than the anal withholding as a metaphor for stinginess. In the classical conception, it is thus the body that is superordinate, while in the other conception, it is the character trait that is superordinate. In yet another complex twist, an originally *somatically* grounded withholding *can come to be* a metaphor for stinginess, but to see stinginess as always and only a derivative of anal withholding is reductive natural science, not hermeneutics.

Obviously the two different positions have major implications for technique. Leo Rangell (1991) began a plenary presentation to the American Psychoanalytic Association with the ringing declaration that "castration anxiety is not a metaphor." I believe it can be both a metaphor and a material reference to the penis. If penis envy can indeed have both material and metaphorical meanings, it seems clear that the analyst's failure to deal with either possibility makes an analysis incomplete. Probably because I am sometimes regarded as neglecting the body, I note with pride that Frank Lossy (1962) won a prize for his report of a case I supervised (when I was a "classical analyst," it is true) in which the successive stages of analysis were marked by a succession of ideationally expressed bodily metaphors. I still believe the work was well done, although I might now place more emphasis on the characterological significance of the fantasies as well.

I am reminded of a delicious (!) cartoon from *The New Yorker*. A cat is leaning against the wall next to a mouse hole in which can be seen a seated mouse with a note pad. They are clearly analyst and analysand. The analyst mouse says, "I wouldn't worry about it. Fantasies of devouring the analyst are quite common." The cartoon vividly portrays the concrete and the metaphorical as well as the two-person character of the analytic situation. As Freud said, intuition can bring up from the depths that which we have to reconstruct so laboriously. Perhaps it will be clarifying to restate that ideas about the body can have material or metaphorical meaning or both, while material bodily manifestations can be metaphorical.

The psychological form in which a metaphor is often represented is as an unconscious fantasy. A typical fantasy, which seems bizarre to nonanalysts, is a woman's belief that she once had a penis but that it was taken away because of some misdeed. Perhaps, if she will only be "good" long enough, she will get it back. In the classical conceptualization, such fantasies are considered to play a leading role in a person's life, exemplifying primary-process thinking. Nonanalytic conceptualizations deny the existence of such fantasies, while nonclassical analysts accept the existence of the fantasies but deny their primary etiological role in personality development. Clearly, neither those who deny their existence nor those who diminish their importance are likely to discover them in their clinical work.

That part of psychoanalysis relating to unconscious bodily fantasies is so idiosyncratically and specifically psychoanalytic that when ego psychology gained ascendence in the 1940s and 50s, some analysts, as I earlier noted, feared that what was truly and particularly psychoanalytic would be lost. And it is true that many case reports that now appear in the literature say nothing about the body, although many others, it is true, say relatively little about anything else. An analyst's theory naturally determines the role he ascribes to the body. Self psychologists, for example, tend to regard manifestly prominent bodily material as secondary to some problem in the cohesion of the self.

I have already given Schafer's description of a Freudian "narrative." Here I will add that it includes three quite distinct categories: body zones with their modes and substances; conceptions of psychic functioning as concretization of these zones with their modes and substances; and familial events during development.

The third category in Schafer's description of the Freudian narrative seems utterly different from either bodily zones, with their modes and substances, or conceptions of psychic functioning as concretization of these zones with their modes and substances. Schafer is referring to such family events as births, deaths, moves, change in economic status, and a host of others. It is this third category of factors that is the usual content of a non-Freudian narrative, while a Freudian narrative is characterized as well by a progressive elucidation of the first two, often unfortunately reductive to the body as concrete rather than seeing conceptions about the body as metaphors as well, with the latter meanings perhaps being the more important. Family events, in Schafer's sense, clearly refers to the psychological meaning of such events, a hermeneutic category.

The conception of the mind as a concretization of zones with their modes and substances as a metaphor is clearly hermeneutic. And the zones themselves with their concrete modes and substances—how do they become psychologically meaningful? In two different ways, corresponding to one-person and two-person psychologies.

In a two-person psychology, bodily functions take place in the context of interpersonal relationships within which they acquire their psychological meanings. If, for example, toilet training takes place in an atmosphere of parental demand and childhood obstinacy, bowel functioning will retain the significance of a battle. Bowel functioning can become a metaphor for any interpersonal struggle because such functioning embraces the concrete zone, mode, and substance in which such a struggle originally took place.

Mitchell (1988) provides an important recent statement of the two-person perspective:

> First, bodily sensations, processes, and events dominate the child's early experience. . . . Second, the fact that sexuality entails an inter-penetration of bodies and needs makes its endless variations ideally suited to represent longings, conflicts, and negotiations in the relation between self and others. . . . Third, the powerful biological surges in the phenomenology of sexual excitement, the sense of being "driven," provide a natural vocabulary for dramatic expression of dynamics involving conflict, anxiety, compulsion, escape, passion and rapture. . . . Fourth, the very privacy, secrecy, and exclusion make it perfectly designed to take on meanings concerning a division of inter-personal realms, the accessible versus the inaccessible, the visible versus the shadowy, surface vs. depth. Sexuality takes on all the intensity of passionate struggles to make contact, to engage, to overcome isolation and exclusion [pp. 102–103].

It is noteworthy how Mitchell silently moves from talking about the body to talking about sexuality. The body is, of course, the more general concept that includes sexuality.

Hoffman (personal communication) makes the important point that Mitchell's discussion seems to restrict bodily functioning to very important interpersonal meanings and thus fails to account for the importance of the body in a one-person psychology. Might there not also be sexual functioning, for example, which is essentially for the pleasure of sexuality itself? The issue is an aspect of the one-person–two-person distinction.

Classical Freudians argue that a hermeneutic position fails to take account of bodily functioning. That need not be so. In a hermeneutic position, the body can and should be taken account of in psychoanalysis, in both theory and practice. But what matters hermeneutically is the meaning of bodily events, not the body as such, that is, not the body as a biological organism. Hermeneutists believe that a change in bodily functioning will be responded to differently, depending on the psychological meaning of the change to the person involved. A mood change resulting from a hormonal change, for example, will elicit different responses depending on what the mood change means to different people. It may be granted that a hormonal change can directly affect mood, since mood can be directly determined physiologically; but how the mood will be experienced is an individual psychological matter. In experiments in which adrenaline, which is released in anxiety, is injected, some persons report that they feel as if they are anxious, even though they know they are not.

Interpersonal theorists regard classical psychoanalytic theory as reductionist because of the ultimate explanatory role given to the body, including bodily functioning as a metaphor. Eagle (1984), who has argued strongly against the hermeneutic position, says that Freud's metapsychology has as its primary purpose the insistence that "because of our genetic-biological structure, certain classes of wishes will universally emerge . . . our biological structure determines the kinds of wishes, aims, and desire we are likely to have" (p. 120). Surely, in a very general sense that is true. Our biological structure, for example, is such that we all have sexual wishes, but the meaning sexuality has to each of us individually is in the psychological realm. Even sexual wishes can be manifestly absent or at least go unrecognized for what they are. Eagle (1984) writes that "how something like a hormonal secretion or hypothalamic stimulation finds its way, so to speak, into our behavior . . . ultimately is at the core of Freud's conception of psychoanalysis as biologically grounded" (p. 120).

I believe the foregoing claim is incorrect. While it is true that Freud's conception of psychoanalysis is "ultimately biologically grounded," it is not true that Freud's concern is with how this biological ground becomes psychologically meaningful. Freud (1925) wrote that the nerve that carries anxiety is of no interest to psychoanalysis. Eagle (1984) argues that a clinical theory-only position limits psychoanalysis to motives, reasons, and aims, and that these are "the very data which themselves require deeper explanation" (p. 149). What does he mean by deeper? He can only mean a biological substrate, for he also writes that "while interpretive explanations in the clinical context may use the personal language of wishes, aims, and feelings, there is no good reason to expect that a theoretical explanation of these wishes, aims, etc. needs to use the same language and the same kinds of concepts" (p. 152). But there is a good reason, and it lies in the rejection of the natural-science level of discourse for psychoanalysis. Freud invited such rejection by noting that his inferences about unconscious mentation were in the same language as his descriptions of conscious mentation, that is, the language of wishes, aims, and feelings.

This is not to deny the importance of research on the way in which body and psyche interrelate, but psychoanalysis can play a role in the elucidation of the interrelationship only insofar as it remains in the realm of wishes, aims, and feelings. It can supply the psychological side of correlations drawn between the psychological and the biological, but that is not to find the "deeper" meaning of the wishes, aims, and feelings. It is to find the biological structure in which they are materialized. A musical composition has the same meaning whether it is recorded in analog or digital form; its deeper meaning will not be found by examining either of these forms of materialization, nor does it reside in the sound waves to which they both give rise.

An interesting glimpse of how Freud (1915–1917) saw the evolving relationship between the biological and the psychological resides in his suggestion that the day might come when the analyst's role would be only to discover by psychological means which pharmacological agent is indicated (p. 436).

DRIVE, EGO, OBJECT, AND SELF AND SUPERORDINACY

One of the remarkable things about the competing psychoanalytic schools is that they all deal with the same kinds of issues. Fred Pine (1990) has recognized this fact and used it to write a book whose very title conveys its message, *Drive, Ego, Object, Self.* Pine's position is that the four variables listed in his title are to be found in all psychoanalytic schools; the differences among them lie in how these four variables are hierarchically arranged. His view is that the hierarchy need not be the same for all people, that any significant psychological phenomenon can be seen in all four issues and that the art of the analyst lies in deciding which should get primacy of attention at any particular point in the analytic process. Gedo (1981) and Lichtenberg (1989) have also proposed that different motives could be in ascendancy at different times in a person's life and, it follows, in different stages of an analysis. The concept of varying hierarchies is not incompatible with a constructivist perspective, although it is not in itself constructivist.

According to these theorists, it is not that analytic material reveals only considerations relating to either ego-id, object relations, or self at any one time. It is, rather, that one of these will seem to be in the foreground at any one time and the others in the background. Obviously the clinical judgment of the therapist will play a significant role in what is considered to be in the foreground or background, underscoring once again that the therapist makes constructions. There is much to commend in this way of looking at things, although the usual reaction of proponents of the various schools is that Pine and his colleagues are endorsing an eclecticism born out of a wish to avoid decisively casting one's lot.

The usual position of each of the four schools is that the variable it primarily emphasizes is explanatory rock bottom and that the other variables appear as preliminary stages on the road toward the true explanation. In classical theory, which with some oversimplification can still be called id or drive theory, ego psychology is an intrinsic part of psychoanalytic theory, while object relations and self psychology, although valuable contributions, must be integrated into the basic id-ego psychology of Freud. By the way, it may not be an accident that it is those aspects of psychoanalytic theory which Freud explicitly labeled that are accepted as basic, namely id and ego psychology. (I am not overlooking that Freud called the superego a differentiating grade within the ego; the term ego psychology really means the id-ego-superego structural psychology.)

Freud's essay on narcissism is as close as he came to referring explicitly to a psychology of the self. It is noteworthy how appropriate it is to use the word self in many places in that essay where he uses the word ego. As I said earlier, Hoffman (in press-a) has said that the classical energy discharge theory hangs by a hair in that essay. The German word for self is *Selbst*. It occurs seven times in the paper as in "self-contentment," "himself," and "self-regard." *Eigene person*, meaning own person, occurs twice. The word self is to be found in "Instincts and Their Vicissitudes" (Freud, 1915) also. Especially noteworthy in this connection is this passage: "Thus we become aware that the attitudes of love and hate cannot be made use of for the relations of *instincts* to their objects, but are reserved for the relations of the *total ego [gesamt ich]* to objects" (p. 137).

Object relations theory and self psychology take a similar position, holding that, while id-ego considerations are important, they must be understood in terms of object relations and self, respectively. Object relations theorists argue that drive is necessarily expressed in terms of object relations, whereas self psychologists argue that drive plays a significant role in pathology only in the context of efforts to shore up a faltering self.

Each school responds to the criticism of other schools by opining that it does indeed take account of the issues that the other schools consider primary. Nevertheless a careful study of the case material offered by each school often shows comparatively little attention to issues regarded as primary by the others. The case book of self psychology edited by Goldberg (1978) seems to me clearly to under-emphasize bodily considerations.

It is important to stress that psychodynamic theories other than psychoanalytic ones are likely to deal with ego, object relations, and self issues but not with the id or, more broadly, the body. In this sense, emphasis on bodily issues is unique to psychoanalysis and makes understandable the classical analyst's concern that any system which does not pay attention to bodily issues or simply no longer makes bodily issues primary is not psychoanalysis, or at least not Freudian psychoanalysis. I believe this is implied in Schafer's description of a *Freudian* narrative, which, I believe, he regards as the best available narrative, his emphasis on constructivist narration notwithstanding.

Where, then, do I stand? My view is that even if drive, object relations, and self are all taken into account, psychoanalytic theory and practice are totally recast—they become radically different from the classical model—if object relations or self is made superordinate to drive. I think the concept of the self is primary, but my discussion of Kohutian self psychology should make it clear that I am not a self psychologist. I did go through a phase in my career when I was an object relationist in reaction against my conviction that classical analysis failed to recognize the two-person nature of the analytic situation. Practicing self psychologists often fail to take issues relating to the body adequately into account. As further examples, I can cite the presentation of a case by the Shanes (1993) and its discussion by Paul Tolpin (1993). A second discussion by Howard Bacal (1993), usually considered a self psychologist, while ascribing hierarchical primacy in the explanation of the case to self issues, did take body issues into account.

For some years now there has been discussion in our literature of "common ground," that is, what psychoanalysts of different schools share in common. Wallerstein (1988) has expressed the view that common ground lies in clinical practice however much the metapsychologies—the theoretical structures of the several schools—differ. This view seems to underestimate grossly the role that theory plays in practice. What the analyst chooses to focus on is heavily dependent on his theory, while what he chooses to focus on directly and centrally influences analytic practice.

Schafer (1993) believes that our diversity is to be celebrated but that the "dark side" of such pluralism is that analysts mingle and confuse the different theoretical systems. Goldberg (1988) argues that to appreciate self psychology truly, one has to practice it wholeheartedly. But then analysts have long maintained that one cannot truly evaluate analysis unless one has been analyzed oneself. Obviously such an argument is akin to the argument that if one is an atheist, it is only because one has not experienced God. Schafer is also opposed to the search for a grand master system to which all analysts can agree, because he regards it as a misguided search for conformity.

Proponents of each system often seem to wish to displace all other systems by their own or at most to afford other systems a subsidiary role. My own position is that the several prominent systems will all find a place in some general system one day with room for hierarchical differences among the several major emphases in individual instances. It will always remain true, however, that both the theoretical predilection and personality of the analyst will be potent factors in the analytic process. The idea of the spontaneous unfolding of the patient's neurosis is a myth. Nevertheless, I also believe that the same major problems in a particular patient will be exposed by any competent analyst.

RESEARCH

Research in psychoanalysis presents many complex problems. It is common to decry the absence of research. Does this absence mean that no advances have been made in psychoanalytic theory and practice? What can we say of the changes for which Freud is responsible? Is the shift from the topographic to the structural theory an advance? Was it the result of research? Is self psychology an advance, even if it is granted that self psychology undervalues drive psychology? Are the changes from monadic to a combined monadic–dyadic viewpoint as described in this monograph an advance? Were they the result of research? Should research be equated with whatever leads to new knowledge, or must work conform to certain methods before it has the right to be called research?

Research in the physical sciences has certainly come to be defined by adherence to what is called the scientific method. Hypotheses must first be established, but in many instances they seem to be the sudden, intuitive hunches of gifted investigators rather than the result of prescribed systematic methods. Then, primarily by the exercise of logic, it must be decided what kind of data are necessary to validate or invalidate the hypothesis. Control groups are required. Elaborate statistical methods have been developed to decide not merely whether or not a hypothesis has been validated, but to what degree one can be sure that the results are not due to chance. There are rules as to what degree of chance must be ruled out before the scientific community takes the work seriously.

Can psychoanalysis claim such research? What counts as evidence in psychoanalysis? I remember that when my monograph redefining transference appeared, an eminent colleague claimed in a review that I had offered no evidence, even though my monograph was accompanied by a second one providing verbatim accounts of psychoanalytic sessions that I believed demonstrated, or at least illustrated, my thesis. I recall being told by another eminent colleague that my views were dangerous because I was so persuasive. He apparently felt that whatever approval my work achieved was because of some personal quality of my own rather than the merit of the ideas themselves.

I discussed earlier whether a view of psychoanalysis as hermeneutic and constructivist rather than as natural scientific and positivist means that it cannot be a science at all. Clearly, whether or not we call something a science has a great deal to do with connotation, not merely denotation. What we are finally concerned with is not whether psychoanalysis can be called a science, but whether we can claim that psychoanalysis can achieve progressive advances in human knowledge. But how shall we measure that?

Some aspects of psychoanalysis seem more readily measurable than others. There is always the struggle between the significant and the exact. Shall we look under the street light because there is more light there even though our keys were lost in the dark alley? We can count and compare the specific words spoken by analyst and analysand, but to what end? We know that the content of a single sentence spoken by an analyst can be of great importance. But will its importance not be a function of the context in which it is said, including whether it is an isolated remark or part of a whole system of interaction?

It is customary to distinguish between process research and outcome research. With the increasing reluctance of third-party payers to finance analysis, demonstration of the value of psychoanalysis by outcome research seems to have become imperative. But how shall we measure outcome? There is much talk of structural change in contrast to the allegedly easily lost symptomatic change afforded by presumably less effective methods of psychological therapy. Whatever complaints one may have about "managed care," the challenge to put up or shut up is salutary.

Outcome research without accompanying process research is of limited usefulness. The fact of an improvement, by whatever criteria, says relatively little unless one also studies how that improvement has come about. Our thinking about a "transference cure" as against a cure by the resolution of a conflict with insight has become more complex with the recognition of the role of new experience in all analysis.

Outcome research could employ the usual methods of control group and statistical evaluation, but work at Tavistock by David Malan (1963) suggests that effective outcome research seems to be best done by comparing the before and after status of each individual case. That analysis is a lengthy process makes outcome research more difficult. Perhaps a study of the patient's status along the way instead of studying only end results can alleviate the problem of the length of analysis. The kind of psychoanalytic therapy I have advocated in this work may make outcome (and process) research easier. There seems to be a persistent belief among analysts that long periods in which nothing much seems to be changing is not inconsistent with a final good result. I would argue than unless an analytic situation as I have defined it is present or at least progressively developing, it is not reasonable to anticipate a good outcome if nothing much is happening.

As Hartvig Dahl (1988) has long maintained, a first step toward process research is to concentrate on the development of methods to do it. It is better to spend our energies in developing such methods than to carry out ambitious studies with methods of unproven worth. Of course pilot studies using a given method are necessary to establish its probable worth.

In my opinion, process research should be done with some kind of recording of the original exchange. I believe that transcripts of audio recordings will suffice. This of course means that nonverbal cues, both vocal and movement, will be lost, but, in my judgment, such cues are usually unnecessary for a judge to develop a plausible conception of what is going on. I am ambivalent about whether reports by the therapist as to what he thinks is going on and why he does what he does are necessary for good process research. On one hand, I do find in supervision that I understand better what is going on when I have the supervisee's account of how he sees what is going on and why he does what he does or refrains from a possible action. On the other hand, Hoffman and I (Gill and Hoffman, 1982; Hoffman and Gill, 1988a, b) concluded that the method we developed for studying the patient's experience of the relationship could produce useful results even when all we had to work with was the transcribed audio recording. (Neither one of us had the temperament or the inclination to work further with the method after we had developed it, but some others [Horwitz and Frieswyk, 1980; Church, 1993] have done some promising studies with it.)

The choice of variable is, of course, one crucial problem of process research. In line with our decision to focus on the significant rather than to be exact, and also in line with our interest in the interaction, we worked with the patient's experience of the relationship, an altered view of what is usually called transference. If one uses significant process variables, judges or raters will have to be psychoanalytically knowledgeable. Another major problem in process research is to determine the unit with which the judge is to work. This problem too implicates the issue of significant versus exactness. Units ranging all the way from a word to a session have been employed. It may prove expedient for one group of raters to determine the units of analysis and another group to do the ratings on the basis of these predetermined units.

The prospects for process research are brightened by the repetitiveness of the interaction. This is in line with the clinical wisdom that a therapist is not likely to recognize a particular interaction until it has been repeated a number of times. A supervisor will commonly say to a supervisee who has missed an interaction, "Don't worry. It will happen again."

The idea that a proper study of process demands a study of each session, and in the original sequence as well, would seem to make the study of a lengthy analysis formidable indeed. But the repetitiveness of the interaction, which also emphasizes the fact that the analyst is often not consciously aware of it, makes sampling feasible. An interesting method reported has been to see whether a judge can arrange sessions taken at random from an analysis into correct chronological sequence. The inability to do so suggests a chaotic or nonprogressing analysis. What may be misleading about focusing on isolated sessions is that patient and analyst can develop catch words for a repetitive phenomenon that a judge may not understand in a single session under review.

Another grave problem in studying process is that a patient's response to an analyst's intervention may not appear at once but only some time later. Furthermore, and this applies not only to a response to an intervention, much in the interaction is expressed implicitly rather than explicitly, underscoring once more the need for psychoanalytically trained judges.

A hopeful development is that a group of about a dozen process researchers are banding together to try to get funding for a research project in which each will apply his or her respective research methods to the same clinical material. A dispiriting obstacle to process research, and indeed to any systematic research in analysis, is that there are so few positions for full-time researchers and so little recognition that such research does indeed demand full-time investigators. With the present decline in the public prestige of psychoanalysis, the prospects for systematic research are not likely to improve anytime soon.

The development of the computer has raised the possibility of a new kind of research. Since the computer can rapidly sort great quantities of words, it may be possible to develop vocabularies that are indices to clinical phenomena and thus to study more rapidly the voluminous verbal material of an analytic treatment. Of course, such research would require the study of the same material by sophisticated clinicians. Work of this sort was pioneered by Dahl and is being conducted at Ulm in Germany (Dahl, Kächele, and Thomä, 1988) and by Wilma Bucci in America.

It is false to conclude that a change to a hermeneutic-constructivist-interactive view of psychoanalysis is an abandonment of the possibility of systematic research. Microscopic study of the interaction between patient and analyst in relation to changes in the patient's psychic state can surely expose repetitive patterns and thus enable decisions among alternative theories. Without such study, analysis will remain doomed to the reiterated positions of the proponents of different theories with no hope of resolution. The latter eventuality does not mean that there will be no change; it does mean that change will come about only as new ideas slowly persuade more and more members of the profession. The outside world demands more. It insists on some systematic validation of specific claims. But analysis should support such work not simply because of the external pressure but for its own scientific advancement. David Rapaport said that many will have to try for a few to succeed.

I close this section by reiterating that there are two kinds of research in psychoanalysis, the systematic kind and the work of clinicians. All the advances—or more cautiously, all the new ideas—in psychoanalytic practice and theory have come from the latter. Other forms of psychological therapy have also been uninfluenced by systematic research, even though some behavior therapists incorrectly claim that their methods arise from, and are validated in, the laboratory.

10

Conclusion

The changes from a natural science to a hermeneutic science and from positivism to constructivism embody a new a metapsychology that supplants Freud's physicoenergic framework. While these changes favor a coherence rather than a correspondence theory of truth, the dichotomy between the two is often too sharply drawn. A pragmatic view in which one's theory is constructivist but in which one works as though correspondence is possible may seem to be fudging principles, but it is the necessary stance of the clinician. The consequences of this stance for research, especially systematic research, have yet to be worked out. It is not clear how hypotheses are to be tested for validity.

On a more specific level, psychoanalysis is to be understood not as of a one-person psychology but as a situation that combines monadic and dyadic features. One might express this by saying that both drive and object relations have to be taken into account, although drive, as used here, does not mean the Freudian metapsychological conception of drive. In less specific terms, the innate and the experiential are always working together. The relationship between the two is not merely additive, as it is in Freud's complemental series; rather, the two shape each other within the constructivist paradigm. The distinction between psychic and material reality remains paramount. A phenomenon is not understood psychoanalytically until its subjective significance to the two participants has been explored.

The analytic situation is one of continuing interaction between the two participants. An overriding consideration in technique is the exploration of this interaction. The hermeneutic-constructivist-interactive model inevitably leads to a redefinition of the received concept of transference. Instead of being defined as the distortion of the analysand's experience of an objective analyst as a result of the analysand's accustomed patterns of interpersonal relationships, trans-

155

ference becomes the analysand's plausible experience of the relationship. It is based on the contributions of both participants to the
here-and-now interaction as well as on their respective past experiences. Analogously, the countertransference is the analyst's experience of the relationship based on the contributions of both participants to the here-and-now interaction as well as on their respective
past experiences.

Although the analysis of the interaction is the central proximal
principle of technique, such analysis often leads to a clarification of
the patient's development, which is clarified in a progressively unfolding and changing narrative. Although the narrative is constructed
by both participants, it is pragmatically viewed as significantly corresponding to the analysand's actual development. The analytic process
can be dialectically viewed as progressive as well as regressive.

But it is not merely transference that is redefined. I cannot think of
any major analytic concept that emerges unscathed from the
hermeneutic-constructivist-interactive framework. Free association
and resistance are jointly constructed. Neutrality no longer denotes
an objective, uninvolved analyst; instead, it points to an affectively
involved analyst who must constantly be alert to his contribution to
the interaction, the redefined countertransference. What is mutative
is not solely insight but insight in the context of new experience. This
insight is into how new experience differs from the old as well as how
the analysand has been shaped by developmental experiences.

Recognizing the inevitability of interaction frees the analyst to be
more spontaneous, rather than misguidedly overly inhibited for fear
of engaging in interaction. It is taken for granted that much interaction is unwitting and recognized only retrospectively. Resistance
remains a central concept, but instead of being seen primarily as an
inhibition of an impulse, it is seen primarily as a contribution to the
interaction that must be understood as a communication.

An analytic process, which may also be called the analytic situation, may be said to exist when both participants accept the idea that
the interaction is central, that both contribute to it, and that the
primary aim of treatment is to understand the patient's contribution
and his experience of the analyst's contribution. For his part, the
analyst will openmindedly and seriously consider the analysand's view
of the analyst's contribution, without binding himself to agree with
the patient's view of the analyst's contribution nor necessarily re-

vealing his own experience and dynamics. But the patient *does* bind himself to reveal as fully as possible his conscious subjective experience and to openmindedly and seriously consider the analyst's view even if it differs from his own. In this important sense, the analytic situation remains asymmetrical.

I have argued that an analytic situation can develop even if the patient is seen less frequently than is usual in psychoanalysis proper. More important, I believe that an analytic situation should almost always be attempted. If the therapist decides it is clearly impossible with a particular patient, he should resort to more overtly supportive therapy, but he should neither prejudge the issue nor give up too easily. It is my experience that therapists often fail to develop an analytic situation because they are too easily put off by a patient who is averse to examining the interaction. Many therapists are faint-hearted in this regard because they are still under the spell of the injunction against interaction by those who do not see the inevitable ubiquity of interaction.

I believe the therapist's identity as an analyst will be safeguarded if he practices psychoanalysis not only via psychoanalysis proper but via the therapy he must undertake with altered extrinsic dimensions. He will thus avoid the twin dangers of attempting to maintain a stiff analytic reserve in his "psychotherapy" on one hand and infusing witting unanalyzed interaction into his psychoanalysis proper on the other. I have suggested that the form of therapy I have described in this monograph be called "psychoanalytic therapy," whatever its extrinsic arrangements. Doubtless, "psychoanalysis" will continue to be used for psychoanalytic therapy, joined with frequent sessions and the use of the couch. I hope that the distinction I have drawn between psychoanalytic psychotherapy as usually practiced and psychoanalytic therapy as I have defined it will be persuasive.

And, finally, although there are also many social and economic reasons for the decline in prestige and practice of psychoanalysis, I am convinced that the absence of systematic research is a major factor contributing to that decline. Let me repeat: We may be satisfied that our field is advancing, but psychoanalysis is the only significant branch of human knowledge and therapy that refuses to conform to the demand of Western civilization for some kind of systematic demonstration of its contentions. While it is true that systematic research in psychoanalysis presents major obstacles, a pitifully small percentage of work in our field is devoted to the development of methods that will allow for informed selection among our competing claims. I intend no belittling of the importance of what has been and is learned from the thoughtful practice of analysis, an occupation that Leo Stone (1961) characterized as carried out by the unaided human heart and mind.

References

Alexander, F. (1956), *Psychoanalysis and Psychotherapy*. New York: Norton.

Apfelbaum, B. (1966), On ego psychology: A critique of the structural approach to psychoanalytic theory. *Internat. J. Psychoanal.*, 47:451–475.

_____ & Gill, M. (1989), Ego analysis and the relativity of defense: Technical implications of the structural theory. *J. Amer. Psychoanal. Assn.*, 37:1071–1096.

Arlow, J. (1975), Discussion of paper by M. Kanzer, The therapeutic and working alliances. *Internat. J. Psychoanal. Psychother.*, 4:69–73.

Aron, L. (1991), Working through the past, working toward the future. *Contemp. Psychoanal.*, 27:81–109.

Bacal, H. W. (1993), Sharing femininity—An optimal response in the analysis of a woman by a woman: Commentary on the Shanes' case study of Kathy K. In: *The Widening Scope of Self Psychology: Progress in Self Psychology, Vol. 9*, ed. A. Goldberg. Hillsdale, NJ: The Analytic Press, pp. 81–85.

_____ & Newman, K. (1990), *Theories of Object Relations: Bridges to Self Psychology*. New York: Columbia University Press.

Balint, M. (1953), *Primary Love and Psychoanalytic Technique*. New York: Liveright.

_____ & Balint E. (1939), On transference and countertransference. *Internat. J. Psycho-Anal.*, 20:223–230.

Basch, M. (1976), The concept of affect: A reexamination. *J. Amer. Psychoanal. Assn.*, 24:759–777.

Berger, L. (1985), *Psychoanalytic Theory and Clinical Relevance*. Hillsdale, NJ: The Analytic Press.

Bergler, E. (1938), On the resistance situation. *Psychoanal. Rev.*, 25:170–186.

Blum, H. (1986), Countertransference and the theory of technique. *J. Amer. Psychoanal. Assn.*, 34:309–328.

Bollas, C. (1987), *The Shadow of the Object: Psychoanalysis of the Unthought Known*. London: Free Association Press.

Bowlby, J. (1969). *Attachment and Loss*. New York: Basic Books.

Brenner, C. (1969), Some comments on technical precepts in psychoanalysis. *J. Amer. Psychoanal. Assn.*, 17:333–352.

_____ (1979), Working alliance, therapeutic alliance, and transference. *J. Amer. Psychoanal. Assn.*, 27:137–158.

Breuer, J. & Freud, S. (1893–1895), Studies on hysteria. *Standard Edition*, 2. London: Hogarth Press, 1955.

Bruner, J. (1993), Loyal opposition and the clarity of dissent. *Psychoanal. Dial.*, 3:11–20.

Busch, F. (1993), Some ambiguities in the method of free association and their implications for technique. Presented at meeting of American Psychoanalytic Association, May.

Church, E. (1993), Reading the transference in adolescent psychotherapy: A comparison of novice and experienced therapists. *Psychoanal. Psychol.*, 10:187–205.

Curtis, H. (1979), The concept of therapeutic alliance: Implications for the "widening scope." *J. Amer. Psychoanal. Assn.*, 27:159–192.

Dahl, H., Kächele, H. & Thomä, H., ed. (1988), *Psychoanalytic Process Research Strategies*. New York: Springer.

Dewald, P. (1972), *The Psychoanalytic Process*. New York: Basic Books.

Dickes, R. & Papernik, D. (1977), Defensive alteration of consciousness: Hypnoid states, sleep, and the dream. *J. Amer. Psychoanal. Assn.*, 25:635–654.

Dilthey, W. (1924), Ideen uber eine beschreibende und zergliedernde Psychologie. *Gesammelte Schriften 5*. Leipzig: Teubner.

Dowling, S., ed. (1991), *Conflict and Compromise: Therapeutic Implications*. Madison, CT: International Universities Press.

Dupont, J., ed. (1988), *The Clinical Diary of Sándor Ferenczi*. Cambridge, MA: Harvard University Press.

Eagle, M. (1984), *Recent Developments in Psychoanalysis*. New York: McGraw-Hill.

Edelson, M. (1988), *Psychoanalysis: A Theory in Crisis*. Chicago: University of Chicago Press.

Eissler, K. (1950), The Chicago Institute of Psychoanalysis and the sixth period of the development of psychoanalytic technique. *J. Gen. Psychol.*, 42:103–157.

_____ (1953), The effect of the structure of the ego on psychoanalytic technique. *J. Amer. Psychoanal. Assn.*, 1:104–141.

_____ (1963), *Goethe: A Psychoanalytic Study, 1775–1786*. Detroit, MI: Wayne State University Press.

Epstein, G. (1976), A note on a semantic confusion in the fundamental rule of psychoanalysis. *J. Philadelphia Assn. Psychoanal.*, 3:54–56.

Fast, I. (1992), The embodied mind: Toward a relational perspective. *Psychoanal. Dial.*, 2:389–409.

Fenichel, O. (1941), *Problems of Psychoanalytic Technique*. New York: Psychoanalytic Quarterly.

_____ (1953), *The Collected Papers of Otto Fenichel*. New York: Norton.

Fliess, R. (1954), The autopsic encumbrance. *Internat. J. Psycho-Anal.*, 35:8–12.

Frank, K. (1993), Action, insight, and working through. *Psychoanal. Dial.*, 3:535–578.

Freud, A. (1954), The widening scope of indications for psychoanalysis: Discussion. *The Writings of Anna Freud*, 4:356–376. New York: International Universities Press, 1968.

_____ (1956), *The Ego and the Mechanisms of Defense*. *Writings 2*. New York: International Universities Press, 1966.

Freud, S. (1895), Project for a scientific psychology. *Standard Edition*, 1:295–343. London: Hogarth Press, 1966.

_____ (1900), *The Interpretation of Dreams*. *Standard Edition*, 4. London: Hogarth Press, 1953.

_____ (1905), Three essays on the theory of sexuality. *Standard Edition*, 7:130–243. London: Hogarth Press, 1953.

_____ (1910a), Five lectures on psychoanalysis. *Standard Edition*, 11:3–55. London: Hogarth Press, 1957.

_____ (1910b), A special type of object choice. *Standard Edition*, 11:165–175. London: Hogarth Press, 1957.

_____ (1912a), Types of onset of neurosis. *Standard Edition*, 12:229. London: Hogarth Press, 1957.

_____ (1912b), The dynamics of transference. *Standard Edition*, 12:97–108. London: Hogarth Press, 1958.

_____ (1912c), Recommendations on analytic technique. *Standard Edition*, 12:109–120. London: Hogarth Press, 1958.

_____ (1912d), On the universal tendency to debasement in the sphere of love. *Standard Edition*, 11:179–190. London: Hogarth Press, 1957.

_____ (1913), On beginning the treatment. *Standard Edition*, 13:123–144. London: Hogarth Press, 1959.

_____ (1914a), Remembering, repeating, and working through. *Standard Edition*, 12:145–156. London: Hogarth Press, 1958.

_____ (1914b), On narcissism. *Standard Edition*, 14:67–102. London: Hogarth Press, 1957.

_____ (1915), Instincts and their vicissitudes. *Standard Edition*, 14:117–140. London: Hogarth Press, 1957.

_____ (1916), Parapraxes. *Standard Edition*, 15:60–79. London: Hogarth Press, 1963.

_____ (1916–1917), Introductory lectures on psychoanalysis. *Standard Edition*,, 15,16. London: Hogarth Press, 1963.

_____ (1918), From the history of an infantile neurosis. *Standard Edition*, 17:3. London: Hogarth Press, 1955.

_____ (1919), Lines of advance in psycho-analytic therapy. *Standard Edition*, 17:158–122. London: Hogarth Press, 1955.

_____ (1920), Beyond the pleasure principle. *Standard Edition*, 18:7–64. London: Hogarth Press, 1955.

_____ (1921), Group psychology and the analysis of the ego. *Standard Edition*, 18:69–143. London: Hogarth Press, 1955.

_____ (1923), Remarks on the theory and practice of dream-interpretation. *Standard Edition*, 19:109–124. London: Hogarth Press, 1961.

_____ (1925), An autobiographical study. *Standard Edition*, 20:7–76. London: Hogarth Press, 1959.

_____ (1926), The question of lay analysis. *Standard Edition*, 20: 177–250. London: Hogarth Press, 1959.

_____ (1931), Female sexuality. *Standard Edition*, 21:223–243. London: Hogarth Press, 1961.

_____ (1937a), Analysis terminable and interminable. *Standard Edition*, 23:216–254. London: Hogarth Press, 1964.

_____ (1937b), Constructions in analysis. *Standard Edition*, 23:255–270. London: Hogarth Press, 1964.

_____ (1940), An outline of psychoanalysis. *Standard Edition*, 23:144–207. London: Hogarth Press, 1964.

Gedo, J. (1993), *Beyond Interpretation* (rev. ed.). Hillsdale, NJ: The Analytic Press.

———— (1981), *Advances in Clinical Psychoanalysis*. New York: International Universities Press.

———— & Goldberg, A. (1973), *Models of the Mind: A Psychoanalytic Theory*. Chicago: University of Chicago Press.

Gergen, K. (1985), The social constructionist movement in modern psychology. *Amer. Psychol.*, 40:266–275.

Ghent, E. (1989), Credo: The dialectics of one-person and two-person psychologies. *Contemp. Psychoanal.*, 25:169–211.

Gill, M. (1954), Psychoanalysis and exploratory psychotherapy. *J. Amer. Psychoanal. Assn.*, 2:771–797.

———— (1963), *Topography and Systems in Psychoanalytic Theory*. New York: International Universities Press.

———— (1976), Metapsychology is not psychology. In: *Psychology versus Metapsychology*, ed. M. Gill & P. Holzman. New York: International Universities Press, pp. 71–105.

———— (1979). The analysis of the transference. *J. Amer. Psychoanal. Assn.*, 27 (suppl.):263–288.

———— (1982), *Analysis of Transference, Vol. I, Theory and Technique*. New York: International Universities Press.

———— (1983). The point of view of psychoanalysis: Energy discharge or person? *Psychoanal. Contemp. Thought*, 6:523–552.

———— (1984), Psychoanalysis and psychotherapy: A revision. *Internat. Rev. Psychoanal.*, 11:161–179.

———— (1988), Converting psychotherapy into psychoanalysis. *Contemp. Psychoanal.*, 24:262–274.

———— (1991), Indirect suggestion: A response to Oremland. In: *Interpretation and Interaction: Psychoanalysis or Psychotherapy?* by J. D. Oremland. Hillsdale, NJ: The Analytic Press, pp. 137–163.

———— (1992). Merton Gill speaks his mind. *Internat. J. Communicative Psychoanal. Psychotherapy*, 7:27–33. Reprint from the *American Psychoanalyst*, 25:17–21, 1991.

———— (1993), Review of E. Levenson's *The Purloined Self*. *Internat. J. Psycho-Anal.*, 74:400–403.

———— (1994a), Heinz Kohut's self psychology. In: *A Decade of Progress: Progress in Self Psychology, Vol. 10*. Hillsdale, NJ: The Analytic Press, pp. 197–211.

———— (1994b), Review of S. Dowling's *Conflict and Compromise Formation*. *Psychoanal. Quart.*

———— (1994c), Letter to the editor re Levy and Inderbitzen on neutrality. *J. Amer. Psychoanal. Assn.*, 42:681–684.

———— & Hoffman, I. Z. (1982), A method for studying the analysis of aspects of the patient's experience of the relationship in psychoanalysis and psychotherapy. *J. Amer. Psychoanal. Assn.*, 30:137–168.

———— & Muslin, H. (1976), Early interpretation of transference. *J. Amer. Psychoanal. Assn.*, 24:779–794.

———— & Wallerstein, R. (1991), An exchange of letters to the editor. *Internat. J. Psycho-Anal.*, 72:159–166.

Glover, E. (1931), The therapeutic effect of inexact interpretation. In: *The Technique of Psychoanalysis.* New York: International Universities Press, 1955, pp. 353–366.

—— (1955), *The Technique of Psychoanalysis.* New York: International Universities Press.

Goldberg, A., ed. (1978), *The Psychology of the Self.* New York: International Universities Press.

—— (1986), Reply to discussion of "The Wishy-Washy Personality." *Contemp. Psychoanal.*, 22:387–388.

—— (1988), *A Fresh Look at Psychoanalysis: The View from Self Psychology.* Hillsdale, NJ: The Analytic Press.

—— (1990), *The Prisonhouse of Psychoanalysis*, Hillsdale, NJ: The Analytic Press.

Gray, P. (1982), "Developmental lag" in the evolution of technique for psychoanalysis of neurotic conflict. *J. Amer. Psychoanal. Assn.*, 30:621–655.

Greenacre, P. (1954), Practical considerations in relation to psychoanalytic therapy. *J. Amer. Psychoanal. Assn.*, 2:671–684.

Greenberg, J. (1986), Theoretical models and analytic neutrality. *Contemp. Psychoanal.*, 22:87–106.

—— (1991), *Oedipus and Beyond.* Cambridge, MA: Harvard University Press.

—— & Mitchell, S. (1983), *Object Relations in Psychoanalytic Theory.* Cambridge, MA: Harvard University Press.

Greenson, R. (1965), The working alliance and the transference neurosis. *Psychoanal. Quart.*, 34:155–181.

—— (1974), The decline and fall of the fifty-minute hour. *J. Amer. Psychoanal. Assn.*, 22:785–791.

Grünbaum, A. (1984), *The Foundations of Psychoanalysis.* Berkeley: University of California Press.

Guidi, N. (1993), Unobjectionable negative transference. *The Annual of Psychoanalysis*, 21:107–124. Hillsdale, NJ: The Analytic Press.

Habermas, J. (1971), *Knowledge and Human Interests.* Boston: Beacon Press.

Hamilton, V. (1993), Truth and reality in psychoanalytic discourse. *Internat. J. Psycho-Anal.*, 74:63–79.

Harlow, H. (1958), The nature of love. *Amer. Psychol.*, 13:673–685.

Hartmann, H. (1948), Comments on the psychoanalytic theory of instinctual drives. In: *Essays on Ego Psychology.* New York: International Universities Press, 1964, pp. 69–89.

—— (1964), *Essays on Ego Psychology.* New York: International Universities Press.

Heimann, P. (1950), On counter-transference. *Internat. J. Psycho-Anal.*, 31:81–84.

Hermann, I. (1936), Sich anklammern . . . zu Suche gehen. *Internat. Zeitschrift. Psychoanal.*

Hoffman, I. Z. (1983), The patient as interpreter of the analyst's experience. *Contemp. Psychoanal.*, 19:389–422.

—— (1987), The value of uncertainty in psychoanalytic practice. *Contemp. Psychoanal.*, 23:205–215.

—— (1991), Discussion: Toward a social-constructivist view of the analytic situation. *Psychoanal. Dial.*, 1:74–105.

—— (1992a), Some practical implications of a social-constructivist view of the psychoanalytic situation. *Psychoanal. Dial.*, 2:287–304.

—— (1992b), Expressive participation and psychoanalytic discipline. *Contemp.*

Psychoanal., 28:1–15.

_____ (1994), Dialectical thinking and therapeutic action in the psychoanalytic process. *Psychoanal. Quart.*, 63.

_____ (in press-a), Review of J. Greenberg's *Oedipus and Beyond. Psychoanal. Dial.*, 5(1).

_____ (in press-b), The intimate authority of the analyst's presence. *Psychoanal. Quart.*

_____ & Gill, M. (1988a), A scheme for coding the patient's experience of the relationship with the therapist (PERT): Some applications, extensions, and comparisons. In: *Psychoanalytic Process Research Strategies*, ed. H. Dahl et al. New York: Springer, pp. 67–98.

_____ & _____ (1988b), Critical reflections on a coding scheme. *Internat. J. Psycho-Anal.*, 26:291–299.

Horwitz, L. & Frieswyk, S. (1980), The impact of interpretation on the therapeutic alliance in borderline patients. Presented at meeting of American Psychoanalytic Assn., December.

Inderbitzin, L. & Levy, S. (in press), On grist for the mill: External reality as defense. *J. Amer. Psychoanal. Assn.*, 42(3).

Jacobs, T. (1990), The corrective emotional experience. *Psychoanal. Inq.*, 10:433–454.

_____ (1991), *The Use of the Self*. New York: International Universities Press.

Kanzer, M. (1966), The motor sphere of the transference. *Psychoanal. Quart.*, 35:522–539.

_____ (1972), Superego aspects of free association and the fundamental rule. *J. Amer. Psychoanal. Assn.*, 20:246–266.

_____ (1975), The therapeutic and working alliances. *Internat. J. Psychoanal. Psycho-ther.*, 4:48–68.

_____ (1980), Freud's "human influence" on the Rat Man. In: *Freud and His Patients*, ed. M. Kanzer & J. Glenn. New York: Aronson, pp. 232–240.

Kardiner, A. (1977), *My Analysis with Freud*. New York: Norton.

Kernberg, O. (1976), *Object Relations Theory and Clinical Psychoanalysis*. New York: Aronson.

Klein, G. (1970), *Perception, Motives and Personality*. New York: Knopf.

_____ (1973), Two theories or one? *Bull. Menninger Clin.*, 37:99–101.

_____ (1976), *Psychoanalytic Theory: An Exploration of Essentials*. New York: International Universities Press.

Klein, M. (1975), *Envy and Gratitude and Other Works: 1946–1963*. New York: Delacorte.

Kohut, H. (1959), Introspection, empathy, and psychoanalysis. *J. Amer. Psychoanal. Assn.*, 7:459–483.

_____ (1971), *The Analysis of the Self*. New York: International Universities Press.

_____ (1977), *The Restoration of the Self*. New York: International Universities Press.

_____ (1984), *How Does Analysis Cure?* ed. A. Goldberg with P. Stepansky. Chicago: University of Chicago Press.

Kris, E. (1956), On some vicissitudes of insight in psychoanalysis. *Internat. J. Psycho-Anal.*, 37:445–455.

Lacan, J. (1977), *Ecrits*. New York: Norton.

Langs, R. (1979), *The Therapeutic Environment*. New York: Aronson.

Laplanche, J. (1987), *Nouveaux Fondements pour la Psychanalyse*. Paris: Presses Universitaires de France.

Levenson, E. (1991), *The Purloined Self*. New York: William Alanson White Institute.

Levy, S. & Inderbitzin, L. (1992), Neutrality, interpretation and the therapeutic intent. *J. Amer. Psychoanal. Assn.*, 40:989–1012.

Lewin, B. (1954), Sleep, narcissistic neurosis and the analytic situation. *Psychoanal. Quart.*, 23:487–510.

_____ (1955), Dream psychology and the analytic situation. *Psychoanal. Quart.*, 24:169–199.

Lichtenberg, J. (1983), *Psychoanalysis and Infant Research*. Hillsdale, NJ: The Analytic Press.

_____ (1989), *Psychoanalysis and Motivation*. Hillsdale, NJ: The Analytic Press.

_____ & Galler, F. (1987), The fundamental rule: A study of current usage. *J. Amer. Psychoanal. Assn.*, 35:47–76.

Lipton, S. (1977), The advantages of Freud's technique as shown in his analysis of the Rat Man. *Internat. J. Psycho-Anal.*, 58:255–274.

_____ (1982), Critical review of Paul Dewald's *The Psychoanalytic Process*. *Contemp. Psychoanal.*, 18:349–364.

Little, M. (1951), Counter-transference and the patient's response to it. *Internat. J. Psycho-Anal.*, 32:32–40.

Loewald, H. (1960), On the therapeutic action of psychoanalysis. *Internat. J. Psycho-Anal.*, 41:16–33.

Loewenstein, R. (1963), Some considerations on free association. *J. Amer. Psychoanal. Assn.*, 11:451–473.

_____ (1971), Panel report: The basic rule: Free association - A reconsideration. *J. Amer. Psychoanal. Assn.*, 19:48–109.

Lossy, F. (1962), The charge of suggestion as a resistance in psychoanalysis. *Internat. J. Psycho-Anal.*, 43:448–467.

Macalpine, I. (1950), The development of the transference. *Psychoanal. Quart.*, 19:501–539.

Mahler, M. (1968), *On Human Symbiosis and the Vicissitudes of Individuation*. New York: International Universities Press.

Malan, D. (1963), *A Study of Brief Psychotherapy*. New York: Plenum.

Marohn, R. C. & Wolf, E. S., ed. (1990), The "corrective emotional experience" revisited. *Psychoanal. Inq.*, 10(3).

Masson, J. (1984), *The Assault on Truth*. New York: Farrar, Straus & Giroux.

McLaughlin, J. (1987), The place of transference: Some reflections on enactment in the psychoanalytic situation. *J. Amer. Psychoanal. Assn.*, 35:557–582.

Menninger, K. (1958), *Theory of Psychoanalytic Technique*. New York: Basic Books.

Mitchell, S. (1988), *Relational Concepts in Psychoanalysis*. Cambridge, MA: Harvard University Press.

_____ (1993), *Hope and Dread in Psychoanalysis*. New York: Basic Books.

Modell, A. (1990), *Other Times, Other Realities*. Cambridge, MA: Harvard University Press.

Namnum, A. (1976), Activity and personal involvement in psychoanalytic technique. *Bull. Menninger Clin.*, 40:105–117.

Olinick, S. (1980), *The Psychotherapeutic Instrument*. New York: Aronson.

Oremland, J. (1991), *Interpretation and Interaction: Psychoanalysis or Psychotherapy*. Hillsdale, NJ: The Analytic Press.

Parker, B. (1965), Father child interaction patterns. *Internat. J. Psycho-Anal.*, 46:332–341.

Pine, F. (1990), *Drive, Ego, Object, Self*. New York: Basic Books.

Psychoanalytic Inquiry (1990), The "corrective emotional experience" revisited. 10:285–458.

Racker, H. (1968), *Transference and Countertransference*. New York: International Universities Press.

Rangell, L. (1991), Castration. *J. Amer. Psychoanal. Assn.*, 39:3–24.

Rapaport, D. (1951), *Organization and Pathology of Thought*. New York: Columbia University Press.

———— (1957), The theory of ego autonomy. In: *The Collected Papers of David Rapaport*, ed. M. Gill. New York: Basic Books, pp. 722–744.

———— (1960), On the psychoanalytic theory of motivation. In: *The Collected Papers of David Rapaport*, ed. M. Gill. New York: Basic Books, pp. 853–915.

Renik, O. (1993), Analytic interaction: Conceptualizing technique in light of the analyst's irreducible subjectivity. *Psychoanal. Quart.*, 62:553–571.

Ricoeur, P. (1981), *Hermeneutics and the Social Sciences*, ed. & trans. J. B. Thompson. Cambridge: Cambridge University Press.

Rogers, C. (1951). *Client-Centered Therapy*. Boston: Houghton Mifflin.

Rorty, R. (1993), Centers of moral gravity. *Psychoanal. Dial.*, 3:21–28.

Rubinstein, B. (1976), On the possibility of a strictly clinical psychoanalytic theory. In: *Psychology versus Metapsychology*, ed. M. Gill & P. Holzman. New York: International Universities Press.

Sandler, J. (1976), Countertransference and role-responsiveness. *Internat. Rev. Psychoanal.*, 3:43–48.

———— (1983), Reflections on some relations between psychoanalytic concepts and psychoanalytic practice. *Internat. J. Psycho-Anal.*, 64:35–46.

———— Dare, C. & Holder, A. (1973), *The Patient and the Analyst*. London: Allen & Unwin.

———— & Sandler, A-M. (1983), The "second censorship," the "three box model" and some technical implications. *Internat. J. Psycho-Anal.*, 64:413–425.

Schafer, R. (1976), *A New Language for Psychoanalysis*. New Haven, CT: Yale University Press.

———— (1979), On becoming an analyst of one persuasion or another. *Contemp. Psychoanal.*, 15:345–360.

———— (1983), *The Analytic Attitude*. New York: Basic Books.

———— (1985), Wild analysis. *J. Amer. Psychoanal. Assn.*, 33:275–300.

———— (1992), *Retelling a Life*. New York: Basic Books.

———— (1993), Discussion of "Theory in Vivo." *Internat. J. Psycho-Anal.*, 74:1163–1167.

Schwaber, E. (1992), Psychoanalytic theory and its relation to clinical work. *J. Amer. Psychoanal. Assn.*, 40:1039–1058.

Shane, E. & Shane, M. (1993), Sex, gender, and sexualization. A case study. In: *The Widening Scope of Self Psychology: Progress in Self Psychology, Vol. 9*, ed. A. Goldberg. Hillsdale, NJ: The Analytic Press, pp. 61–74.

Slavin, M. & Kriegman, D. (1992), *The Adaptive Design of the Human Psyche*. New York: Guilford Press.

Spence, D. (1993), The hermeneutic turn: Soft science or loyal opposition. *Psychoanal. Dial.*, 3:1–10.

Spezzano, C. (1993), *Affect in Psychoanalysis: A Clinical Synthesis*. Hillsdale, NJ: The Analytic Press.

Stein, M. (1981), The unobjectionable part of the transference. *J. Amer. Psychoanal. Assn.*, 29:869–892.

Stolorow, R., Brandschaft, B. & Atwood, G. (1987), *Psychoanalytic Treatment: An Intersubjective Approach*. Hillsdale, NJ: The Analytic Press.

Stone, L. (1961), *The Psychoanalytic Situation*. New York: International Universities Press.

Sullivan, H. (1940), *Conceptions of Modern Psychiatry*. New York: Norton.

—— (1953), *The Interpersonal Theory of Psychiatry*. New York: Norton.

—— (1964), *The Fusion of Psychiatry and Social Science*. New York: Norton.

Sulloway, F. (1983), *Freud: Biologist of the Mind*. New York: Basic Books.

Tansey, M. & Burke, W. (1989), *Understanding Countertransference: From Projective Identification to Empathy*. Hillsdale, NJ: The Analytic Press.

Thomä, H. (1993), Training analysis and psychoanalytic education: Prospects for reform. *The Annual of Psychoanalysis*, 21:3–75. Hillsdale, NJ: The Analytic Press.

Tolpin, P. H. (1993), Primary failures and secondary formations: Commentary on the Shanes' case study of Kathy K. In: *The Widening Scope of Self Psychology: Progress in Self Psychology, Vol. 9*, ed. A. Goldberg. Hillsdale, NJ: The Analytic Press, pp. 75–79.

Tomkins, S. (1981), The quest for primary motives. *J. Pers. Soc. Psychol.*, 41:306–329.

Wachtel, P. (1977), *Psychoanalysis and Behavior Therapy: Toward an Integration*. New York: Basic Books.

Waelder, R. (1930), The principle of multiple function. *Psychoanal. Quart.*, 15:45–62, 1936.

Wallerstein, R. (1986), *Forty-two Lives in Treatment*. New York: Guilford Press.

—— (1988), One psychoanalysis or many? *Internat. J. Psycho-Anal.*, 69:5–21.

—— (1989), Psychoanalysis and psychotherapy: An historical perspective. *Internat. J. Psycho-Anal.*, 70:563–591.

—— (1990), The corrective emotional experience: Is reconsideration due? *Psychoanal. Inq.*, 10:288–324.

White, R. (1959), Motivation reconsidered: The concept of competence. *Psychol. Rev.*, 66:297–333.

Wilburn, D. (1979), Freud and the inter-penetrating of dreams. *Diacritics*, 9:98–110.

Winnicott, D. (1971), *Playing and Reality*. London: Tavistock.

Wolf, E. (1988), *Treating the Self*. New York: Guilford Press.

Zetzel, E. (1956), Current concepts of transference. *Internat. J. Psycho-Anal.*, 37:369–376.

—— (1970), *The Capacity for Emotional Growth*. New York: International Universities Press.

Index

169